CLASSROOM MANAGEMENT

A GUIDE FOR URBAN SCHOOL TEACHERS

Sean B. Yisrael

ROWMAN & LITTLEFIELD EDUCATION

A division of
ROWMAN & LITTLEFIELD PUBLISHERS, INC.
Lanham • New York • Toronto • Plymouth, UK

Published by Rowman & Littlefield Education
A division of Rowman & Littlefield Publishers, Inc.
A wholly owned subsidiary of The Rowman & Littlefield Publishing Group, Inc.
4501 Forbes Boulevard, Suite 200, Lanham, Maryland 20706
http://www.rowmaneducation.com

10 Thornbury Road, Plymouth PL6 7PP, United Kingdom

British Library Cataloguing in Publication Information Available

Library of Congress Cataloging-in-Publication Data
Yisrael, Sean B.
 Classroom management : a guide for urban school teachers / Sean Yisrael.
  p. cm.
 ISBN 978-1-61048-762-7 (cloth : alk. paper) — ISBN 978-1-61048-763-4 (pbk.
: alk. paper) — ISBN 978-1-61048-764-1 (ebook)
 1. Classroom management—United States. 2. Education, Urban—United
States. 3. Students with social disabilities—United States. I. Title.
 LB3013.Y55 2012
 371.102'4—dc23

                                                          2011047882

∞™ The paper used in this publication meets the minimum requirements of
American National Standard for Information Sciences—Permanence of Paper
for Printed Library Materials, ANSI/NISO Z39.48-1992.

Printed in the United States of America

CONTENTS

FOREWORD

It's truly an honor and a privilege to write this foreword on behalf of Dr. Sean Yisrael. I've had the pleasure of knowing Dr. Yisrael for several years as a colleague and personal friend. I can honestly say that Dr. Yisrael is truly one of the most passionate education professionals I have ever know. Throughout his career, he has worked tirelessly to serve students, parents, and his community. His career is a testament to his hard work and commitment to impact the lives of students and provide a quality education for those who are underprivileged.

To truly understand what drives him and the motivation that fuels his work, it is helpful to know of his humble beginnings. Sean was raised in poverty, the eldest of five siblings. His mother, a single parent, worked two jobs to support her family. This placed a lot of responsibility on her eldest son. The community he grew up in was plagued with violence, drugs, and crime. Sean experienced many hardships as a child, but he was able to overcome them and get an education.

Unlike most education scholars who merely write about issues and problems in education, Dr. Yisrael is someone who has actually experienced them. His perspective is unique and vastly different from those of his contemporaries. He has walked in the shoes of those whom he serves, which makes his writings and commentary more authentic and informative. His personal background gives him greater insight on the issues that affect urban and inner city youth and the type of schools they attend. Dr. Yisrael is also aware of how to better resolve the issues that can transform public education so that all public school students, regardless of their families' economic status, can receive a quality education.

Classroom Management: A Guide for Urban School Teachers is a guide that teachers can truly follow to transform their classrooms. Since Dr. Yisrael's early life once resembled the life of today's urban students, this book puts the reader in tune with the conditions urban students face (in and outside of school) and how those conditions shape teachers' and students' behaviors within the classroom. The strategies mentioned will help new as well as experienced urban school teachers establish and maintain order in their classrooms. They will also gain knowledge on how to effectively deal with some of the most challenging student behaviors. After reading this book, teachers will spend less time dealing with behavioral issues and more time on academic issues. In my opinion, this is a must read for every teacher who works in any urban metropolitan school district in America.

Dr. Carlos Blair

INTRODUCTION

In 2005, while working as an administrator in an urban school district located in southwestern Ohio, I observed a teacher while conducting one of my many informal classroom visits. This particular teacher was twenty-five years old, had graduated at the top of her class with an English degree, and had obtained her teaching certification. This was her first teaching position, and she was having a tough time. Her particular struggles were not due to incompetence because she was very knowledgeable of the content. The teacher's difficulties were due to her lack of classroom management skills.

Over the span of my career (sixteen years and counting), I've encounter many teachers whose poor classroom management skills adversely affected the quality of instruction they were able to deliver to students and seriously hindered their abilities to maintain employment as a teaching professional. Year after year, teacher after teacher, classroom after classroom, I have observed various teachers with similar classroom management issues. It doesn't matter if the teacher is new to the profession or a so-called veteran—classroom management is an area of concern for many teaching professionals.

The problems are intensified when it comes to teaching in an urban school district. I say this because the dynamics of the urban school landscape is extremely hard for most teachers to contend with, regardless of their years of experience. For example, most urban school districts have a very high concentration of students who come from poor or low-socioeconomic families. These families (and the students thereof) are as diverse as the neighborhoods they come from. In these neighborhoods, there is a high concentration of crime, gang violence, drugs, teenage pregnancy, domestic and child abuse, unemployment, child neglect, untreated mental illness, and single-parent households. These types of environmental attributes make living in these communities tough, to say the least. This affects the school's environment because not only do students bring a lot of their families' social baggage to school with them, but there are also a lot of community issues that find their way into the school building.

Another aspect of the urban school landscape is the problem of recruiting and maintaining highly qualified teachers. Many qualified and experienced teachers are opting to take jobs in private, rural, or suburban school districts where the student population is more homogeneous (i.e., same ethnic background, similar income level and social status, certain level of parental support, same value system, etc.). These school districts tend to have fewer students with behavioral problems, and they present less challenges to learning. This leaves the urban or inner city districts with an oversaturation of inexperienced teachers. I'm not saying that hiring an inexperienced teacher is a bad thing, because truly every good teacher was inexperienced in the beginning. But compounding this problem is that at the same time this is happening, many veteran urban school teachers are retiring or leaving the profession altogether.

One of the greatest enigmas of urban education is the issue of classroom management. It is the main reason new teachers have problems and why experienced teachers leave the profession. There have been many books and articles written on the topic, but very few are truly geared toward the actual experiences of the urban school teacher. Most textbooks written on the topic merely discuss best practices and strategies teachers should use and cite sources from "experts" and others who have contributed to the profession. A little further research into the backgrounds of some of these so-called experts would reveal that many of them have never taught in an urban or inner city school, and in some cases, they have never worked in any school district—urban or otherwise. Many have collegiate careers or they're the pseudoscientific types who reference quantitative studies or hash out statistics to back their preconceived ideologies about what urban schools need. Although one may acquire some form of knowledge from books written from such authors, the depth of these books is very limited.

A high percentage of the classroom management books on the market today tend to be very generic and do not genuinely resonate with the true experiences of urban school teachers and the students they serve. The generic nature of most classroom management books for urban educators is directly related to the writers' lack of experience in dealing with urban or inner city students. Their detached perspective causes their work to be flat and not altogether linked to the actual challenges faced by urban educators in the classroom.

A good portion of the books on the topic are written from the outside looking in, instead of the other way around. A person who has never been in a war can't write a book on the topic from the same perspective as someone who has served in one. The person who has actually experienced warfare firsthand can deliver more accurate and vivid descriptions of the experience because he or she has been in the trenches with mud on his or her face and gun in hand. This person has heard (and possibly felt) the bullets, felt the pursuit of the enemy, and seen the carnage and the aftermath of war.

Classroom management takes on an entirely different meaning when teaching in an urban school district. I'm writing from a perspective that is directly linked to the topic in multiple ways (personal, professional, and academic). I am someone who was born in generational poverty.

My mother was the youngest of four siblings, raised in a single-parent, female-governed household. My mother, like all but one of her siblings, never knew her biological father. I was born when my mother was sixteen years old. By the time she was thirty, she had given birth to a total of five children from three different men, all of whom were absentee fathers who didn't support their children. The neighborhoods I lived in lacked adequate housing, employment, and safety. They were plagued by crime, gangs, drugs, and a host of other societal ills.

I attended schools that were considered to be low performing by the standards of the state where I lived. They too mirrored the same detrimental issues that affected the neighborhood I lived in. It was only by the blessings of the Most High that I was able to overcome such obstacles and pursue a college education. After college, I returned to my high school alma mater to teach social studies, coach basketball, and serve as a mentor and after-school tutor.

Upon returning as a teacher, I immediately noticed how the level of disruptive student behaviors had increased from the time when I was a high school student, making a teacher's ability to manage a classroom even more critical. After working as a teacher for seven years, I decided to turn my focus toward school administration. As of the writing of this book, my administrative work has been in urban school districts. Becoming a school administrator gave me an expanded view of school operations and enlightened me on the various types of student misbehaviors and why certain types of behaviors occurred. The expanded view of classroom management issues in the classroom became the catalyst for my research and the foundation for this book.

The point I'm trying to make is that I'm writing about classroom management for urban teachers because I've truly lived it. The knowledge I share within the pages of this book was acquired from intense involvement, active participation, and years of research. I too have studied the "experts" and reference relevant sources, but more important, my education and personal background have given me the ability to make the strategies I've learned connect with the real experiences of urban school teachers, making this book more organic, authentic, and visceral.

Classroom Management: A Guide for Urban School Teachers delivers the reasoning behind what makes urban or inner city students tick and how such information will lend itself to improved classroom management. Readers will learn the tricks of the trade from the inside out, instead of the distant collegiate view of outside in. This book will prepare any urban school educator, regardless of his or her experience level, for the challenges faced when trying to manage successfully the most challenging urban school classrooms. It doesn't matter which grade or subject matter of the teacher. The strategies in this book will arm teachers with a comprehensive set of skills to enable them to get the job done, because they will know which critical areas on which to focus.

I not only discuss how to handle behavior problems associated with the most extreme students, but I also discuss the other areas least recognized for having an impact on classroom management (i.e., learning what students' lives are like outside of school, forming relationships with parents, creating an environment conducive to learning, creating effective lesson plans, etc.). Some of the strategies will cause the reader to think outside the box, while other strategies are merely best practices that can be used in any school setting (urban, suburban, private, rural, etc.). But most important, the reader will learn how to link the strategies to fit directly the needs of the students being served. In the end, I hope you will find this book to be the ultimate urban teachers' guide to classroom management.

1

UNDERSTANDING THE BIG PICTURE OF URBAN EDUCATION

Classroom management is, and always will be, one of the most talked about topics in education. With the advent of federal legislation such as No Child Left Behind and increased emphasis on high-stakes testing and standards-based education, a teacher's ability to effectively manage the classroom becomes even more vital. According to Groves (2009), classroom management can be defined as the actions teachers take to create an environment that supports and facilitates both academic and social-emotional learning. It encompasses more than just dealing with student behavioral issues; it also deals with how well a teacher organizes the learning activities, maintains order and safety, establishes daily routines and practices, and implements classroom procedures while still delivering quality instruction.

Whenever a judgment is made on a teacher's effectiveness, the first thing that is usually considered is how well the teacher manages the classroom. Administrators and parents alike want to know: Are students well behaved? Are students listening and responding appropriately to the teacher? Does the teacher have enough control and order over the class as a whole? With classroom management being such an important issue, I find it ironic that most universities that offer teacher education programs spend very little time on this subject.

Most aspiring teachers receive the bulk of their teacher training around educational theory, ethics, lesson planning, and curriculum development and implementation. A very small percentage of their educational training is devoted to classroom management because the university student is expected to learn classroom management in the field during his or her few weeks of student teaching or gain such knowledge from on-the-job training. This becomes problematic for new teachers because they leave many universities with a bachelor's degree in education, but lack proper knowledge to effectively perform a very critical aspect of the job.

I'm not advocating that areas of study such as ethics, curriculum development, theory, lesson planning, and other topics are not important because they truly are, but there should be more time devoted to the importance of classroom management. This is especially true for teachers who will teach in urban districts after graduation. Student teaching is not the best means for an aspiring urban teacher to gain classroom management skills for a couple of reasons.

First, student teaching is usually done at the end of the teaching program as one of the last requirements before graduation, which is partly the reason why so little time is devoted to this subject. Second, the time designated for student teaching is also devoted to the development of other skills (i.e., lesson plan development, instructional delivery, collaborative planning, experiencing school culture, implementing learning strategies, etc.). Depending on the student-teaching situation, little to no time will be directly allocated for learning specific skills that will help with classroom management and all that is involved with it.

Furthermore, a significant portion of the teachers who teach in urban school districts do not perform their student teaching in urban school settings. The main reason for this is that most universities with teacher education programs generally establish relationships with nonurban schools or school districts, so most of their students' practical experience will come from one type of setting (i.e., rural, suburban, or affluent schools). I don't think the university officials are intentionally being biased toward urban schools, but their desire is to connect with school districts that are high performing or rated effective by the state.

The universities want their students to experience what it's like in the high-performing districts in hopes that some of that "high performance" will rub off on their students. Establishing relationships with high-performing school districts also helps to give the universities more credibility when selling their teacher education program. The selling points for the universities sound a lot better when they can say they have relationships with high-performing school districts, as opposed to mentioning those with a bad reputation or a history of failure.

The reality is that the number of teaching positions in highly effective school districts is minimal. When a teaching vacancy opens in these kinds of districts, they often get hundreds of applications for one position. School officials in affluent districts can hire the cream of the crop, which is usually not a first-year teacher right out of college. A few novice teachers may get lucky enough to get hired, but the vast majority of them will have to seek employment in other school districts, and many of them will find themselves in urban school districts where the demand for teachers is usually high. Since many of the universities don't have relationships with urban school districts, their students will not be exposed to the realities of the urban teaching experience. This will ultimately put them at a great disadvantage when they begin working. These teachers will have to get their experiences through on-the-job training.

Even though there are a lot of positive aspects about on-the-job training, it still is not the most effective way for all teachers to learn classroom management skills because it puts the teacher in a position of having to sink or swim. All teachers will go through periods of trial and error until they have become comfortable in their teaching and classroom management abilities. Classroom management and the management of students' overall conduct are skills that teachers acquire and hone over time. These skills almost never "come together" until after a minimum of two to three years of teaching experience (even more so with some teachers). Effective teaching requires considerable skill in managing myriad tasks and situations that occur in the classroom each day.

With proper support from school administrators, teacher mentors, professional developers, coaches, and collaborative planning, novice teachers can weather the storm and stay afloat until they become secure in their abilities to manage their classrooms successfully. In many public school districts across the country, especially urban school districts, the personnel needed to assist novice teachers are either lacking or nonexistent. Most new teachers who work in urban school districts will not have a mentor, coach, or assistant teacher to work with them on a consistent basis. Unless the building principal is proactive and develops a teacher mentor program within the school building or a natural relationship is formed with a veteran teacher, the novice urban school teachers will generally have to tackle classroom management alone.

Without the proper support, it is almost impossible for novice teachers to be successful in the area of classroom management, which will have devastating implications on the quality of education their students receive. During the period of trial and error, the novice teacher could quickly experience a loss of morale and confidence if his or her initial tactics to gain control over the classroom do not work. According to a case study on job satisfaction conducted by the National Center for Education, student misbehavior was one of the major causes for low teacher morale and feelings of burnout (Lumsden, 1998). Novice teachers need a complete understanding of what to do on the first day of school, not three or four years into their careers.

Having a teacher in a classroom who doesn't have a solid understanding of how to properly manage the class is like having a certified mechanic who is not comfortable with working on a car's engine. The mechanic knows what a car engine is and the importance of this vital part to the car's performance, but he doesn't know how to deal with a problem associated with it. Not having knowledge of how to maintain or repair an engine can have adverse implications for other parts of the car (i.e., transmission, battery, gears, pumps, radiator, alternator, driving performance, lifespan of the car, etc.), impair his ability to properly maintain the parts he does have knowledge of, and hinder the owner's ability to use the vehicle.

A mechanic in such a position could be nothing more than ineffective because he lacks the skills to perform one of the most vital functions of his job. Until the mechanic learns the skills needed to repair a car's engine, he will not be able to remain in the profession very long. He will eventually go out of business once word spreads about his lack of knowledge and ability. The same scenario also holds true for teachers and their ability to manage their classrooms.

Many teachers, especially novice ones who start their careers in urban school districts, are in the same predicament as the mechanic in my example. Being unable to effectively manage a classroom can also adversely affect other areas of a teacher's performance. Ineffective classroom management skills will greatly impact the quality of instruction delivered to students (i.e., lesson planning, class assignments and activities, student learning, test scores, etc.) and lead to the teacher having feelings of being burnt out, self-doubt, and low self-efficacy.

If teachers don't feel good about going to work each day, then they will not feel good about the students they're working with, nor will they care about the quality of work the students produce. Raising a teacher's morale will not only make the act of teaching more pleasant for the teacher, but it will also make learning more pleasant for the students; lowering a teacher's moral level can have the reverse affect (Wood and McCarthy, 2002).

Having worked in several urban school districts as a high school administrator, I've had the opportunity to work closely with many novice teachers. When meeting with a new teacher for the first time, I always ask the teacher which aspects of the job present the most problems for him or her. In almost every instance, the topic of classroom management is always mentioned first. It is also the area where teachers have the most anxiety before starting a new school year.

Most teachers usually feel confident in their abilities to teach and deliver quality instruction, but their greatest fears are connected to how well they'll be able to establish order and deal with everyday behaviors of students and situations as they occur. When dealing with urban teachers with three or more years of experience, they often claim student behavior as the number one factor plaguing the school or their individual classrooms, which indirectly points to issues associated with classroom management.

Teachers with varying degrees of experience need assistance with classroom management because most never learned to properly deal with student misbehaviors. Due to their lack of exposure to urban school–related issues at the university level, coupled with not having a mentor or advisor when being employed within an urban school district, many veteran teachers gain bad habits and often contribute to the dysfunction that happens within the classroom. If a teacher never learns how to deal effectively with various student misbehaviors, it will greatly compromise his or her ability to deliver quality instruction to students and adversely affect the teacher's ability to maintain employment. For teachers who work in urban school districts, having this ability takes on an entirely different meaning.

An urban school district is one that constitutes or encompasses a city or town whose schools are administered by a local school board located in a metropolitan area (McAdams, 2000). The word "urban" is normally used instead of or associated with such words as inner city, central city, downtown, metropolitan, nonrural, ghetto, or business district. Most urban school districts service a very diverse population (i.e., race, gender, family income level, handicap, etc.).

The greatest difference between urban districts versus their private, suburban, or rural counterparts is the high concentration of minority students who come from families of low socioeconomic status, meaning families who live below the poverty line. The Center for American Progress reported that in 2007 students who lived below the poverty line in the United States lived in families of four whose annual household income did not exceed $15,000 per year (www.americanprogress.org). Some rural districts may have high numbers of students who come from families who live below the poverty line, but those students are usually more homogeneous, having the same ethnic background, community values, language, and so forth.

Urban families who live below the poverty line are usually more diverse. The students who attend urban districts vary in race, income, social norms, beliefs, community, and sometimes language. Students from such families have different needs, disabilities, environmental issues, and learning barriers that are in direct contrast to students who come from average rural, middle-class, or affluent families.

For teachers who work in urban districts, classroom management takes on an entirely different meaning because they face different challenges. The same classroom management techniques that would work in a classroom within a private, suburban, or rural school district may not necessarily work in a classroom within an urban school district. You could take a highly qualified and effective veteran teacher with a history of good classroom management and producing high-achieving students from a suburban or private school and put him or her in an urban classroom teaching the same subject and grade level and using the same methods and strategies with contrastingly different results.

I'm not saying suburban, private, or rural school teachers don't face challenges in regard to managing their classrooms, nor am I advocating that all suburban students are well behaved and the urban students are not. What I am saying is that due to the diverse nature of most urban school districts, the teaching and learning barriers associated with urban students become inherently different, and at times more difficult than their suburban, rural, or private school counterparts.

School districts are as uniquely diverse as the communities they serve. According to Hill and Celio (1998), schools are an extension of the community. Urban districts with a high concentration of low socioeconomic students generally serve the most challenging students. These students come from communities that are deprived of the basic resources required to stay vibrant and flourishing. Such communities typically have high unemployment rates, substandard housing, poor sanitation, high concentrations of drug distribution and addiction, inadequate health care, and higher crime rates than suburban and rural neighbors.

Most urban communities across America breed a culture of violence: domestic, gang related, and abuse against children and women. Most of these students come from single family homes headed by one parent. Students who live in low socioeconomic communities generally have parents or relatives who didn't have successful educational experiences themselves. Because of this, education is devalued and not regarded as a top priority within the home or community. The overall attitude of the people living in these communities is that of despair, hopelessness, and a general distrust for the law and others who are in a position of authority. They feel locked out of the "American Dream" and don't believe that the "system," in any form, be it governmental or educational, will work for them.

By no means am I generalizing or making assumptions about a group of people based on where they live or their socioeconomic status. There are many honest, hard-working, and law-abiding people who live in low-economic urban communities. These parents want the best for their children just as do other concerned parents who live in affluent communities, but the element I previously described is real and does exist as a prevalent part of the communities in which many urban students live. By ignoring the existence of these conditions and how they affect the urban classroom, any legitimate attempts of successful classroom management or proper education of the urban student are negated.

In many urban communities, the values and beliefs, assumptions, ways of communicating, and the rules for survival are different from middle-class and affluent communities. According to Payne (2005), there are various hidden rules for survival among the social classes in America. These hidden rules determine what's important for people, and from an educational standpoint, have great implications on teaching and learning in the school setting.

One example is how people in different classes communicate when dealing with a conflict. According to Payne (2005), being able to fight or to have someone able to fight for you is crucial to survival in poverty, but with the middle class, being able to use words in debate or as tools to negotiate is crucial. The middle class typically are taught to handle conflict by having a discussion between the two sides in hopes of coming to some kind of agreeable resolution to the problem. If the discussion becomes heated and tempers flare, then one or both parties will separate by moving into another space or physically leaving the situation altogether.

The parties who are in conflict may come back together after time has elapsed and tempers have cooled off. In some of the more difficult situations of conflict, the middle class will even move to another neighborhood or buy land where daily interactions with neighbors are limited. People who live in poverty have very limited resources, and their living arrangements are usually crowded and cramped. There is usually not a place of solitude in one's own apartment or living quarters, and moving to a secluded place outside the community is not a viable option. Because of the stifling living conditions, the person in poverty will have to fight for any and everything he or she has of value or importance because, if not, it will probably be taken and consumed by someone else.

It is important to understand the contrasts mentioned above because most teachers and education professionals were raised in middle-class, or affluent home environments with the values thereof. In most cases, the people who are teaching in urban school districts don't have the same or similar backgrounds as the students they are serving; neither have they had the same childhood and educational experiences. Many urban education professionals walk into the classroom assuming the values, opinions, interest, and experiences they had as a student will be the same as the urban students they're teaching. Without proper understanding of the urban students' psychological and developmental needs as it relates to their communities and environmental culture, teachers will have an extremely difficult time maintaining order within the classroom.

For example, a few years ago I took a graduate-level course on community engagement and support. One of the students in my cohort gave a personal testimony about how when she was in junior high school, one couple in her small rural community got a divorce. According to my colleague's testimony, the divorce devastated her entire community because the family had a child, who was a personal friend of the person giving the testimony. She went on to say how people in the community rallied behind the family, and the school assisted in providing additional support and resources for the child of the divorced parents.

Another person in the class gave a testimony of when he was in high school, and how the entire school was devastated when one of his classmates (in a class of 600) died in a drunk driving accident. He talked about how grief counselors where provided for students, in addition to other resources that were provided throughout the school year for families who were most affected by the tragedy. Some of the resources, as my colleague proclaimed, were even extended throughout the following school year.

When it was my time to speak, I explained how I (being someone who was raised in generational poverty), and like most of my peers, grew up in a poor inner city area without a father or stable man living in the household. In fact, most of my friends never had the opportunity to see their fathers face to face. One childhood friend of mine had four siblings, all within two years of age of each other. Each child had a different father, whom the children had never met. That was just in one family, but there were others with the same or similar family circumstances and we all went to school together.

I also explained how three of my childhood friends died before age sixteen. One was found floating in the Ohio River with his body severely beaten and his genitals severed from his body, another was shot by a stray bullet at the end of the school day in front of the high school we attended, and another swallowed several grams of crack cocaine while trying to elude apprehension from the police. I also explained how the high school I attended averaged about three student deaths per year. When I finished speaking, everyone in the class was speechless. They were astonished at how I was able to make it to a point in my life where I could even attend a graduate-level education program after having been surrounded by so much turmoil, violence, and adversity.

The members in the cohort had a right to be surprised because a good number of my peers never graduated from high school, let alone made it to a master's or doctorate-level program at a university. My ninth-grade class contained 500 students. By the time I made it to my senior year four years later, only 102 actually graduated. Some died before graduation, while others were incarcerated, but most merely dropped out. The sad part is that what I outlined in my personal testimony is only the tip of the iceberg. There were countless issues that I, and many other urban-educated students, had to face before graduating from high school.

Through it all, I can't remember having any additional support from the school or community members for my family or others like mine. There weren't any grief counselors, psychologist, or therapists to help us transition through our issues of death, loss, or separation. We had to deal with our issues on our own, and we were expected to perform and function on the same level as students who were void of such issues or had the proper support to cope. From a teaching perspective, urban educators must enable their students to achieve the same academic outcomes as those who work in settings where students do not have the same detrimental personal or environmental issues. This is the reality of urban education, and it is this reality that makes classroom management so vexing for urban school teachers.

In the chapters that follow, I will discuss methods that urban teachers can use in order to cope with many of the issues they'll face while working in an urban school district and with urban students. If urban classroom teachers follow the steps outlined, they will be armed with the knowledge to deal with any behavioral issues that may arise in the classroom, therefore making classroom management a nonissue. The teacher will not have to wade several years into his or her career in order to manage the classroom effectively and handle student discipline issues. He or she will be equipped do what is necessary now to be successful.

2

LEARNING WHAT STUDENTS' LIVES ARE LIKE OUTSIDE OF SCHOOL

After reading chapter 1, you should now have a good understanding of why classroom management for urban educators can be problematic, so in this chapter I will discuss what can be done to combat most of these problems. It is true that many teachers, whether urban or otherwise, acquire effective classroom management skills by trial and error during the first few years of their teaching careers, but this doesn't have to be the only way. Teachers can have effective classroom management on the first day of class during their first year of teaching.

Effective classroom management for an urban educator doesn't start when students arrive at the school building. It starts on the very first day when the teacher accepts the position and signs the contract with the school district. This is usually when the teacher is informed of his or her teaching assignment (location of the school, grade level, subject area, etc.). It is then that the teacher should immediately begin to do research on the students he or she will teach to gain an understanding of the cultural environment in which the students live. This is the start of the process and the foundation from which the urban teacher should operate.

According to Wiles and Bondi (1998), an attempt should be made to understand the educational and cultural levels of the community, general attitudes about the school, and expectations for education in the arca. Teachers of urban students need relevant information and a basic understanding of what students' lives are like outside the walls of the school building. For urban school teachers, this would include—but not be limited to—learning the students' psychological, environmental, and community dynamics. This should happen before the teacher takes one step inside the classroom.

Good classroom management skills require that teachers understand, in more ways than one, the psychological and developmental levels of their students (Johnson, Finn, and Lewis, 2005). Furthermore, teachers need to know how factors outside of the school's walls influence students' perceptions and actions inside the school (Weiner, 2003). Knowing such factors will help guide the teacher's decision making. Without this information, urban educators will quickly find themselves in a position of doubt, uncertainty, and unpreparedness.

Most teacher preparation programs at the university level do not offer many opportunities for aspiring teachers to learn the basics of parent and community involvement through their coursework and practicum, nor are they able to gain an understanding of the strengths of the diverse communities that make up poor urban neighborhoods (Johnson, Finn, and Lewis, 2005). Learning the circumstances that impact students' lives outside the school is crucial because it gives the teacher a framework to better understand the students and to build a deeper connection with them. The understanding gained will not only lead the teacher down the path to better classroom management, but will also lead to avenues that will better serve the students' overall needs.

Let's look at how professional sports teams prepare for a big game as an example. Before two teams square off against each other in a contest, they typically will scout the opposing team by sending a representative to one of their opponent's contests against another team. While scouting, the representative will learn the other team's key personnel, their plays and strategies, as well as the opposing team's strengths and weaknesses. The scout will try to learn as much information as possible before reporting back to his own team. The scouting team will take the information learned and use it to devise a winning strategy before the game is played. It will serve urban educators well to start scouting their students before they step into the classroom.

Many educators make the mistake of treating students and the schools they attend as isolated entities. Schools are an extension of their communities; likewise, students are an extension of their families—one cannot be separated from the other. Schools generally reflect many of the characteristics of the society or community in which they're located (Knujufu, 2002). Urban educators must view classroom management from this holistic standpoint.

The majority of teachers and education professionals were not raised in poor urban neighborhoods, and they do live in the same communities as the students they will teach. In most cases, the teacher hasn't had the same experiences as the students they're teaching; neither do they share the same community values and social norms, which can cause a huge disconnect between students and teachers. According to Brown (2003), a high percentage of urban teachers will be, and are, inexperienced middle-class white Americans.

Many teachers in urban districts walk into their classrooms assuming their teaching experiences will be similar to their education experiences or assume students will share the same values and social norms. They make the mistake of thinking the students they will teach will have the same ideas, aspirations, goals, and enthusiasm for school they once had as a student. Without a proper understanding of the students' psychological and developmental needs as they relate to their families, communities, and environmental culture, teachers who work in urban districts will have an extremely difficult time of maintaining order within the classroom and providing a quality education for students (Knujufu, 2002).

DO YOUR RESEARCH

Urban educators can start their research by doing two things: (1) utilizing the Internet and (2) visiting the communities where students live. These two simple tasks will give teachers greater insight and serve as the knowledge base for how they will work to manage their classrooms effectively. In a sense, the teacher is acting like an archaeologist or an anthropologist, searching for artifacts that will give insight into the community and school's cultural past and history.

Starting with the Internet, the teacher should select a search engine like Google or Yahoo! and keyword search the school and the names of the neighborhoods where students live, looking for articles or information within the past ten years. The educator should also look for current community information such as crime statistics (domestic and gang violence, drug abuse, burglaries, homicides, etc.), socioeconomic status (income level of families, poverty, etc.), types of housing (residential homes, public housing, or both), and political and residential events (festivals, relevant elections, town hall meetings, etc.).

In researching the school itself, the teacher should learn information such as graduation rates, suspension rates, student attendance, school traditions, and so forth. A lot of important school information can be found at the public library or on the school district's website. While searching, be very careful of the sources. Take time and filter through the information and stay away from personal blogs, vanity websites, and personal opinion pieces that are not from credible institutions.

After digesting the information gathered on the Internet and through other sources, the next step is to visit the communities. I've learned over my personal experiences that things are not as bad (or as good) as everyone says. In order to know something for sure, I have to check it out myself. I know many urban communities are not the safest places to go, so I wouldn't recommend visiting the communities at night or going alone if you are uncomfortable with that. But I would suggest for a teacher to go alone, with a partner, or in a group during daylight hours. A good idea would be to make a connection with a few teachers in your school building and turn it into a group event. It can be a learning experience for all of the teachers in the school building to share and grow from.

Whether you go alone or with colleagues, it is imperative to make the visit. It will also give you a chance to better evaluate the data gained from the Internet research. Just because you're able to read or view something on the Internet doesn't make it true. There are bloggers who take bits and pieces of information and publish them on their personal vanity sites. You will also find news articles written by reporters who seem to always write negative articles about urban schools and communities, or slant the article in a way that doesn't tell the complete story.

It's up to you to sift through the information and take what you can use and disregard what you cannot. If you are too afraid to visit the communities, then you probably are not suited to work in an urban school setting. If you choose to take a position in an urban district without initiating the above mentioned process, then you are putting yourself in a disadvantaged position.

Without visiting the communities, teachers not only put themselves in a disadvantage position, but they also put themselves at risk of developing what I call a "those people" complex, where a person begins to label or stereotype a group of people whom they're not familiar with. They say things such as, "Can you believe those people? I wouldn't be caught dead around those people. Those people act like animals. Those people are crazy. Those people . . . those people . . ." and so on. People who have this mindset usually have a superiority complex and are usually ignorant of the plight, circumstances, problems, or struggles of the people they're labeling. And since they seldom have the opportunity to really get to know "those people" or walk in their shoes, it is easier for them to pass judgment or to stereotype.

Teachers who work in urban districts can easily fall into this category when they fail to do their research. In the absence of research, teachers fall prey to listening to rumors, speculation, and innuendo about the community, school, parents, and students. They begin to listen to the people who espouse the "those people" philosophy. They hear people say things such as, "The students at this school are this way . . . the students at this school are that way . . . those kids are bad . . . they can't learn . . . the students at this school do not know how to act."

Hearing such negative talk about a school and its students will undoubtedly have a negative impact on a person and change his or her attitude. Instead of the teachers reporting to work with excitement and enthusiasm, they will carry feelings of uncertainty, fear, doubt, and paranoia, causing the first sign of misbehavior to reinforce the negative opinions heard from others. Meanwhile, no significant action is being taken in order to effectively deal with the misbehaviors. One teacher with this kind of mentality can do a lot of damage within a school building, but several can be catastrophic.

Another kind of unprepared teacher frequently seen in urban schools is the naïve teacher. Naïve teachers usually are good hearted, passionate, and want to "save the world." For them, it's not about a paycheck, it's about trying to lift urban students out of their plight of depressed circumstances by providing the gift of education that they've come to deliver. They believe their love for helping children (students) will transform negative situations and circumstances, and that the students will grow and reach new levels they could have never imagined.

Naïve teachers are the ones who are gobbled up the fastest. Their lack of knowledge about their students ill prepares them for the real challenges they will face in the classroom. Within a few months (and sometimes a few days) the naïve teacher will be hanging on out of desperation, and if not properly advised, he or she could seek refuge from negative influences that will ultimately lead to a reduction in the quality of educational services delivered to students.

Visiting the communities where students live is also good for teachers because it takes away some of the fear and anxiety that teachers have when reporting to an urban school (especially if the school has a bad reputation). The teacher will get to see that the people of the community are not as bad as others portray them. The urban teacher will get a chance to see the residents and students of the communities as actual human beings instead of rejects of society. Once you have seen a person's human qualities, it becomes extremely hard to place unbefitting labels on them. The community visit should consist of the teacher(s) walking the neighborhoods, making observations of the people, evaluating the community's landscape, and striking a conversation with some of the residents.

I utilized the above mentioned practices as an urban high school teacher and administrator. The information I learned helped me in both positions tremendously. I walked the communities, went inside local establishments, and even talked to some of the community's residents. I once walked into a mom-and-pop store and introduced myself to the store's manager. I spoke of the school and of my position. Then I politely asked the manager to share with me what he knew about the neighborhood and the school.

You'd be surprised at what a person will tell you if you ask the right questions. The manager and I talked for almost an hour about various aspects of the school, its staff (past and present), and the student body. He even introduced me to an honor roll student who worked part time in the store. I was able to ask the student questions, which provided insight as to how the school was viewed from the student's perspective.

Another example is when I started a conversation with a man who was a deacon at one of the local churches in the community. The deacon and I had a lengthy conversation about the negative impact the gangs and drugs in the neighborhood had on the youth. He told me the names of two gangs in the community that were based out of two housing projects located on opposite ends of the neighborhood. The gangs were at odds with each other because they were fighting to control the drug trade in the community. I learned about the colors each of the gangs wore to identify themselves, their signs and symbols, their initiation practices, and even some past crimes committed due to the gangs' fighting with each other. The conversation was very enlightening because I learned things that weren't available to me via the Internet or the library.

Later, I was able to draw from the information I learned while talking with the deacon because I ended up having several students in my classes who were gang affiliated. One class in particular had two male students from rival gangs. I noticed that one young man had a tattoo of his gang's symbol on his right hand, and the other young man had on a t-shirt with the words "Tot Lot" printed on the front of it. I remembered from my conversation with the deacon that one of the gangs used to hang out at a children's play area near the projects where they lived. The words "Tot Lot" signified that particular gang.

Having the two students in my classroom at the same time was a potentially explosive situation, but my research helped me to deal with it. My initial action was to separate the two students in the classroom. I organized a seating chart, intentionally placing the students on opposite sides of the room. The students thought the separation was coincidental, but it was planned. Something as simple as a seating chart helped to curb potential conflicts.

A teacher who did not have the information I obtain from my research might have sat the students next to each other unknowingly. Friction would have mounted in the room until the students decided to act in an inappropriate manner, leaving the teacher clueless as to why the two students were misbehaving. These types of situations can regularly occur in an urban classroom, and the teacher will be clueless as to why the situations are happening or learn why after the fact, but by then it will be too late.

Second, I incorporated certain tenets of conflict resolution and character building within my lessons. I would often have discussions on how to solve problems without resorting to violence and how to accept others when they are different from you. I would usually start the first ten to fifteen minutes of class with some sort of character-building question as a warm-up.

Third, I also referenced things that I knew about the students' world (places, events, people, etc.) within certain lessons and gave students the opportunity to dialogue, share, present, and converse with me and one another. This kept the students engaged and participating because many of the lessons were related to their interests or things that directly pertained to them. This also let the students know that I was in touch with things that mattered to them and that impressed them. The information gained from my previous research helped me to build rapport with the students in my classes. An increase in the level of rapport leads to a multidirectional flow of ideas as students are encouraged to voice their opinions and derive meaning from the information they share (Gremler and Gwinner, 2008).

I never tried to degrade them or highlight the fact that I knew some students were in a gang. I was able to relate to them on a level that other adults in the school couldn't. Over time, the two students from rival gangs arrived at a point where they could mutually coexist in the same class without having to be separated.

The students may have had differences outside of school, but they were able to put their difference aside while in my classroom. They also recognized and respected my efforts at trying to keep the peace and my role as the classroom teacher to educate them. By complying with the classroom rules, they demonstrated how much they valued their education. There was a mutual understanding and shared respect between the students and the teacher.

MAKING CONNECTIONS

When teachers lack the ability to relate to students, they lose touch with them and never establish genuine rapport or make any relevant connects. This is why learning what students' lives are like outside of school is so vital. It allows the teacher to establish rapport and make deeper connections with students, therefore leading to better classroom management. Establishing rapport with students is probably one of the most overlooked aspects of establishing effective classroom management in urban school districts, yet it is the most critical because it plays a very important role in determining if the class will be successful and enjoyable.

According to Tickel-Degnen and Rosenthal (1990), there are three components in the structure of rapport. I will only discuss the first two because those are the components that are specifically related to how urban educators should seek to establish it. The first component is attentiveness as it relates to a group feeling as one. The mutual circumstances, conditions, situations, and shared experiences will bind the group together, calling for a shift from self-awareness to the awareness of others.

Many teachers in urban districts seldom express oneness with their students. It's hard to create this atmosphere in the classroom when the teacher knows nothing about the students or never takes the time to establish any genuine connects. Their actions, speech, and nonverbal communication with students signal to them that the teacher is not "like us." If the students view the teacher as an outsider, they will not be as willing to comply with the teacher's request or, in some cases, complete assignments or work to be successful in school.

Teachers can establish connections and build rapport with students by learning the students' hobbies, interest, goals, and abilities, or by calling them by a preferred nickname. When I was a classroom teacher, I would have students fill out an identification card that asked certain questions to allow me to gain more information about them. The type of information I requested would not be found in the students' file in the main office. I asked for information that reflected how the students felt about themselves and how they wanted to be viewed by others.

The second component of establishing rapport is creating mutual friendliness and caring. This happens when members of a group perform actions that demonstrate mutual respect, admiration, and concern for one another (Tickel-Degnen and Rosenthal, 1990). Most teachers will say they care about their students, but there are often things that teachers do to indicate otherwise. For example, some teachers never sponsor a club or attend any after school functions. When the school day is over, they get in their automobiles and drive as far away from the school and community as possible.

Teachers who fit the above category put themselves at a great disadvantage compared to the teachers who do stay after school for clubs or school events. When students see teachers after school, or at times outside the regular school day, it communicates to the students that the teacher cares enough to take additional time to be with or to help them. Also, seeing a teacher at a school event like homecoming, prom, open house, or a sporting event allows the student to see the teacher in a different light. The students get a chance to see the teacher as a real person, instead of as a school employee, therefore making it more difficult for the student to misbehave in the teacher's class whom they've just bonded with, or shared a significant moment with, the evening before at an afterschool function.

When I worked as a classroom teacher, I coached basketball, sponsored clubs, provide tutoring after school, and attended school functions. I also attend certain events in the communities surrounding the school. A number of my students were present at one community event I attended. When they saw me, it was as if they had seen a celebrity! They were so excited (and shocked), showing me off to their family members and friends.

I shook a lot of hands that day and was able to speak to several parents, grandparents, aunts, and uncles of many of my students. I was not only able to establish rapport with those students who saw me, but my presence at this community event helped to establish "oneness" with the students, school, and community. Later I learned that the connections I gained with my students became contagious, spreading to other students by word of mouth. Soon, students I didn't even know began to know and respect me and even seek me out when they had a problem. According to Brown (2003), the best urban teachers show warmth and affection to their students and give priority to the development of their relationships with students as an avenue to student growth.

Another way that mutual friendliness and caring can be established with students is through the power of food. Yes, food! I'm not advocating having weekly pizza parties or bribing students with fast food gift cards in exchange for good behavior. Doing this would not only be considered poor practice, but also a gross display of ignorance associated with knowing what students' lives are like outside the classroom.

According to Payne (2005), the hidden rule concerning food (concerning people of low socioeconomic status) is that food is equated with love. When resources and money are low, the distribution and consumption of food takes on an entirely different meaning for those living in poverty. In many cases, food is not only a way to show a person you love him or her, but it also shows forgiveness and feelings of care.

Being privy to this information, urban school teachers can work to create mutual friendliness and caring by strategically implementing food. For example, a teacher might have an after school program or tutoring session after which he or she could serve snacks for all students who attended. Another example would be to arrange for an educational field trip outside of the school. While on the trip, have an appointed time for everyone to sit down and eat together. This is something that is typically overlooked because people who did not grow up in poverty (most teachers) or have limited exposure to those who did do not place high significance on food. It doesn't matter the type of food you serve, but what does matter is the gesture and the connections that are established because of it.

Many urban students are disconnected from the school and its staff mainly because they do not feel any genuine reason to be connected. Urban students in their neighborhood schools generally don't believe teachers actually care about them, trust them, or have their best interests in mind (Weiner, 2003). This happens because many teachers and staff in urban schools don't take the proper time to build genuine connections, mainly because of fear, uncertainty, and doubt. When this happens, it makes it easier for students to misbehave because they don't view the teacher or the school as part of their community (or group). The feeling of "oneness" is totally void.

I believe it is the teachers' responsibility to forge the connection between themselves, students, and the school. According to Weiner (2003), teachers display knowledge of what students' lives are like outside of school by making connections, personal and intellectual, between school learning and lived experiences. In doing so, they will be able to build more significant relationships with students, which is the foundation for effective classroom management.

In today's tough educational climate, in order to reach urban students, teachers must make genuine connections with them. This is done by having access to their inner lives. Teachers must expand their knowledge of their student population and attain as much information as possible—about their inner lives, joys, frustrations, and aspirations. Doing so will give teachers an understanding of how urban students view the world around them, and more importantly, how teachers can work to expand that view. This is vital in order for teachers to have effective classroom management.

CHAPTER SUMMARY POINTS

- Teachers must follow a process and action in a certain way in order to have effective classroom management.
- Teachers must learn what students' lives are like outside the school.
- Use the Internet and visit the communities where students live in order to gain insight to the students' environmental, social, and psychological needs.
- Establishing rapport is vital to effective classroom management.

3

GET RID OF FEAR AND SYMPATHY

I previously worked in urban schools that were considered some of the worst places to work by the local media and by those in and outside the schools' community for those particular areas. I can vividly recall several instances when casual conversations outside of work led to discussions about urban education. When it was discovered that I worked in the field of education and at the particular schools with the bad reputations, the facial expressions of the people with whom I was speaking changed. Some faces would show shock, while others would express sympathy. It didn't matter whether I was speaking with a fellow educator or someone in another profession, the reaction would always be the same. "Wow, you work there? Man, how do you do it? I commend you for working there. Those kids are lucky to have you. I couldn't work there no matter what they paid me."

One such conversation I had was with a friend who was also an educator, but at a private school. This teacher won several accolades during his career, which at the time, spanned over a decade, one of which was a Teacher of the Year award. He was also very active in the school where he worked, spearheading several committees and programs for staff and students. His students always received high scores on state proficiency tests, and he relished in that fact.

Throughout our conversation about our places of employment, he stated that despite his ability and experience as a classroom teacher, he didn't think he could work in the same school where I was working. I probed him to find out why he felt that way. His response shocked me. He responded by saying, "How could I be productive in a place where I would be afraid each day? You can't teach students if you are afraid of them."

My friend was absolutely right. How can a teacher work in a school where he or she is afraid? I believe many teachers of urban children, especially the novice ones, probably share the same sentiments as my friend. Sometimes, educators can let their fears become a major stumbling block to effective classroom management and their ability to deliver quality instruction to urban school-aged students.

Classroom management is more difficult in urban schools than in private, rural, or suburban schools because gaining students' cooperation while ensuring their learning involves addressing students' cultural, ethic, social, identity development, language, safety needs, as well as their academic growth (Brown, 2003). If a teacher is scared of the students whom he or she is commissioned to teach, how will that teacher be able to successfully fulfill the responsibility of addressing all the needs associated with the students?

Fear is a powerfully intrinsic emotion we all have as humans. *Random House Dictionary* (2001) defines fear as a distressing emotion aroused by impending danger, evil, or pain. Many urban teachers, especially novice ones, report to work not having done their research on a school or the community, ill prepared for the challenges that await them.

They've heard rumors and seen short clips on television (some distorted and some true) about the school or community that have caused fear and anxiety to set in. A classroom teacher's fear will manifest itself in ways that are detrimental to students' growth and achievement, causing the teacher to be afraid to hold students accountable, maintain high expectations, contact and converse with parents, make any reasonable attempt at establishing rapport, and the list goes on and on.

The most adverse effect of fear from a teacher's standpoint is that the students will be able to sense it. From the first encounter with the teacher, students will be able to determine if the teacher is afraid of them. If there is any sign of fear in the teacher, the students will attack like a hungry lion after its prey. A fearful urban classroom teacher will lose respect, authority, and overall control of the classroom. As a school administrator, I've encountered many teachers who had classroom management issues where fear was the root cause (fear of not knowing what to do in a given situation, fear of how the students will respond, fear of how parents will react, fear of what colleagues will think, fear of verbal or physical abuse from students, etc.).

FOUR TYPES OF FEARFUL TEACHERS

In the fall of 2006, I conducted a case study involving thirty-six urban high school teachers in two school districts located in southwestern Ohio who were identified as having excellent classroom management. Individual interviews and surveys were done in an effort to identify the common traits these teachers possessed. The data from this study also interestingly revealed common traits these teachers possessed when they were not as effective in their classroom management strategies at various points in their careers.

The most common trait among these teachers during their years of ineffective classroom management was fear. According to the data collected, the fear these teachers possessed caused them to fall into four categories of ineffective classroom managers. I labeled each of the categories according to the characteristics displayed by the teacher. The four categories are (1) the buddy teacher, (2) the blind teacher, (3) the overreactor, and (4) the sympathizer.

The first category, the buddy teacher, is a teacher who wants to be the students' friend. This type of teacher is ineffective because he or she diminishes his or her authority by placing him- or herself on the students' level. The teacher is afraid to take a stance or set any classroom rules for fear of a backlash from students. This teacher will attempt to fraternize with students in order to win their cooperation in the classroom. This approach leads to inappropriate relationships with students and ineffective classroom management because fraternizing blurs the lines of authority between teacher and student.

One particular teacher shared a story with me on how she tried to become buddies with her students instead of assuming the higher level of authority the teacher should possess. She took this approach because she had witnessed several incidents when students were fighting in the halls, and she feared being part of some sort of violent exchange with students, whether directly or indirectly. Trying to become friends with the students was her attempt at effective classroom management, figuring if students liked her, they would not become upset or act inappropriately in class. This led to poor classroom management because she created an atmosphere where the students thought they could get away with things because their "buddy" would look out for them, not send them to the principal, or hold them accountable in any way. Instead of being treated as an authority figure in the classroom, the teacher was viewed as a peer and treated accordingly.

The teacher admitted that all a student had to do was raise his or her voice in a loud tone and she would easily give in to them. She shared a story of how she once let a female student leave the class six different times within the same class period to "use the restroom." On the sixth time the student asked to leave, the teacher declined the student's request because the student had not attempted to do the assignments for the class period. The student yelled at the teacher in a loud tone, "I got to go to the restroom, so give me a pass!" The teacher immediately gave in to the student's request to avoid escalation of the situation. The teacher also shared that the student didn't return to the classroom until the next day. To make matters worse, the teacher didn't notify the principal of the event or contact the student's parents.

The most damaging effect to the teacher in this scenario was that the incident took place in front of the entire class. When students see teachers demonstrate signs of weakness in situations when they should show strength, they will exploit the weakness and transform the teacher's classroom into chaos. Over time, the teachers will find that students in the class who would not have been a behavior problem will begin to show signs of disrespect or become disinterested in the class, creating a domino effect of daily class disruptions and misbehaviors. The end result is that no significant learning will take place in this kind of classroom environment.

The next category, the blind teacher, is one that is very common in a lot of urban school districts. When I say blind, I don't mean in a literal sense. I'm referring to a teacher who never "sees" what's going on in the classroom because he or she ignores inappropriate actions and responses from students. This teacher ignores students' misbehaviors, hoping and praying the students will stop on their own, but they never do. He or she will usually keep on with the lesson or activity, as if someone were paying attention, in hopes that the inappropriate actions of students will eventually cease because the teacher does not want to intervene.

Just like with the teacher who wants to be friends with students, this teacher is also afraid to intervene for fear of a possible backlash from students. This kind of teacher will lose authority and overall control of the class because the students will continue to push and test to see how far they will be able to go. If, or when, the teacher finally decides to respond, it will cause an even greater backlash from students because the response was too late. This kind of teacher is likely to have a major catastrophe in the classroom, and the teacher will be oblivious as to how it happened.

One teacher shared how her actions led to her losing control during the first few weeks of school. Students would come and go out of her classroom as they pleased, use profanity, eat food, refuse to do any class assignments, or participate in the class activities. By the fourth week of school, students were literally throwing books and other items out of the window in plain sight of the teacher and a host of other inappropriate actions. Members of the school's security team and administration would frequently have to visit this teacher's classroom because there was always some kind of disturbance or student behavioral issue.

Ignoring inappropriate actions from students is not the answer to effective classroom management. Addressing misbehavior when it first happens lets all students in the classroom know the teacher's expectations for what is, and is not, acceptable behavior. Failure to do so indicates to students that there are no boundaries for the classroom, so they can do whatever they want whenever they want.

The third category, the overreactor, is one who makes every situation into a state of emergency. Many teachers go through this phase at certain points in their careers, and many more remain in this phase. The overreactor's foundation for effective classroom management consists of putting students out of class for any reason, no matter how trivial or insignificant. The teacher doesn't employ any intervention strategies or methods to handle situations in class.

Putting students out of class for marginal offenses is a way of transferring ownership to someone else, which is usually to the administrators. These types of teachers do not realized that when they transfer ownership of student behavioral issues to another person, they also transfer ownership of authority as well. I like to compare it to a mother whose only method of disciplining her children is to threaten to tell the children's father. When the mother does this, she is indirectly telling the children she is not in control and is unable to handle the situation. She is also communicating to her children that she needs an outside entity (the father) to intervene because she is not equipped to effectively deal with the problem the children have caused. This kind of approach diminishes the mother's authority and transfers power and authority to the father. Even though the children may love their mother, they will have greater respect for their father because he is the person whom they've been reared to obey, respect, and listen to.

Likewise, the classroom teacher who sends students out of class for trivial things will cause students to lose respect for the teacher, therefore, giving respect and authority to the administrator or person handling the issue. Urban teachers need to employ various management strategies within the classroom before sending students out. Most classroom problems can be solved without ever having to send the student out of class. The more issues teachers are able to solve in class, the more they will appear to be in control and capable to the students.

The last category is the sympathizer. Teachers in this category hear about some of the students' home life situations and environmental conditions and they begin to feel sorry for them, therefore lowering their standards and expectations for students. According to Kunjufu (2002), a teacher's expectation is the most important reason why children excel or fail in school. When standards are lowered, the quality of education is lowered and student achievement drops.

One teacher in my case study gave an example of how she used to let her feelings of sympathy adversely affect her judgment. She would make excuses for the students' misbehavior by believing the students were a product of their environment. She was afraid to apply any rules, consequences, or high standards for fear she would be adding too much pressure to the already stress-filled and tumultuous lives led by the students. She later learned her view of gloom, doom, despair, tragedy, and hopelessness was not altogether accurate and definitely not a reason to lower standards and expectations.

ASSERTIVENESS EQUATES TO CONFIDENCE

In order to have effective classroom management in an urban school, the teacher must get rid of all fear and sympathy and replace it with assertiveness and empathy. A teacher's level of assertiveness starts with his or her overall confidence as a professional. Confident teachers are not fearful, nor are they unsure of themselves and their abilities. They have a positive view of themselves, their abilities to educate, and their purpose for being an educator. They understand their responsibilities and feel capable of fulfilling their role.

Assertive teachers react confidently and quickly in situations that require the management of student behavior (Burden, 2003). They give firm, clear, and concise directions to students who are in need of guidance to help them behave appropriately. Students who comply are reinforced in a positive way, whereas those who disobey rules and directions receive consequences. Assertive teachers do not see students as adversaries, but rather as active participants in the overall functioning of the class (Burden, 2003). They react to students in ways that are consistent and nonthreatening.

According to Canter and Canter (2001), assertive teachers build positive, trusting relationships with their students and teach appropriate classroom behavior via direct instruction, describing, modeling, practicing, reviewing, and encouraging through a system of reward. Teachers should appear friendly, but not go as far as trying to become the students' friend. Teachers should be demanding, yet warm with their interactions with students. They should also be supportive and have a respectful, nonthreatening tone when addressing misbehavior. Assertive teachers listen carefully to what their students have to say, speak politely to them, and treat everyone fairly.

The *Random House Dictionary* (2001) defines empathy as identification with the feelings, thoughts, and experiences of another. Empathy should replace sympathy because sympathy will cause the teacher to feel sorry for students, therefore doing a great disservice to them. Urban students do not need educators to feel sorry for them. They need teachers who have knowledge and understanding of their issues, but who will still set high expectations and demand high performance. Feelings of empathy will cause teachers to work harder, and more diligently, to ensure students are receiving the best education possible.

CHAPTER SUMMARY POINTS

- You can't be an effective teacher in an urban district if you are afraid of the students.
- There are four categories of teacher ineffectiveness: the blind teacher, the buddy teacher, the overreactor, and the sympathizer.
- Teacher expectations are the most important reasons why students excel.
- Replace feelings of sympathy with feelings of empathy.
- Urban teachers need to be more assertive and confident.
- Urban students do not need teachers to feel sorry for them.

4

ESTABLISH ROUTINES, PRACTICES, RULES, AND CLASSROOM NORMS

This chapter is what I like to call the nitty-gritty. I've dubbed it as such because it's the nuts and bolts of how effective urban classroom management should be carried out. It combines all the other strategies mentioned previously into an effective classroom management plan. I've broken this chapter into two distinctive parts: (1) establishing routines and (2) dealing with students' misbehaviors. The first half involves how teachers should work to establish routines, practices, procedures, and common norms for governing the class. If urban teachers fail to implement and reinforce routines, common norms, and practices, then the previous steps outlined in the first three chapters will have no effect.

This chapter will discuss how teachers can encourage students to take ownership of their own behavior, so the expectations for students are met automatically. Proper implementation of classroom routines, practices, and procedures will also have great implications on how the teacher deals with students' misbehaviors. The second half of the chapter will advise teachers on how to deal with all levels of student misbehaviors effectively and maintain control of the classroom so teaching and learning can take place.

CLASSROOM ROUTINES, PRACTICES, PROCEDURES, AND NORMS

Effective classroom management is no different from any other activity or sport that requires participants to follow rules in order to be successful. For example, in order to drive on the expressway, all licensed drivers must follow a prescribed set of rules. Drivers must yield to other drivers already on the road before entering, follow the speed limit, and use the left lane for passing. Licensed drivers are made aware of driving rules before receiving a state-approved driver's license, and by the many visible signs and signals posted on the road. Drivers who fail to follow the rules that govern the proper way to drive will suffer consequences. The consequences could range from getting a speeding ticket to being arrested or, worse, causing a fatal accident. Compliance to these rules depends largely on law enforcement's ability to enforce them.

Likewise with classroom management, urban teachers need rules in place so the classroom can operate smoothly and so that students can be aware of the expectations that should govern their behavior. Teachers with ineffective classroom management skills never formally establish classroom norms and practices, and students are never formally told how they are expected to conduct themselves in class; therefore, the expectations are unclear and not firmly rooted.

This is why two teachers who teach the same group of students could see contrasting behaviors in their respective classes. One teacher can gain compliance from students and have little or no behavioral issues, and those same students can wreak havoc in another teacher's class the following period. Classroom norms and practices are an essential part of effective classroom management and necessary for students' ability to learn (Burden, 2003).

Before I discuss how to establish these practices, or even what types of practices to implement, I would like to ask the reader to participate in an exercise that I used to do when I played high school and college basketball. Before every game, and usually when I practiced alone, I would use mental visualization as part of my preparation. Mental visualization is the process of creating a mental picture or intention in your mind that you want to happen or feel (Quinn, 2008).

When I played basketball, I would create mental pictures of my movements, the crowd, actions of my teammates, and even how I would respond to certain game situations before the game was played. I did this because I found that the mental pictures I created in my mind caused me to naturally react when faced in certain games situations. While playing in college, I remember hitting the game winning shot in the final seconds of an important game. When the coach called the play, I was ready and confident that I could do it because I had previously rehearsed taking and hitting a game winning shot a thousand times in my head.

I use my experience with playing basketball as an example, not to boast of any past achievements or to stroll down memory lane, but to provide the urban teacher an example of how to use this technique for classroom purposes. Oftentimes teachers have ineffective classroom management skills because they do not have routines and common practices, but also they never gave any advance thought about how they would strategically respond to certain situations encountered by misbehaving students. Before you can be an assertive and confident urban teaching professional, you have to see yourself as one. If you can't see yourself successfully managing classroom misbehaviors, you never will.

Before the first day of school, urban teachers should mentally visualize how they would like their class to operate. They should envision their students, where they will sit, and how classroom interaction will occur. They should envision how they will deliver instruction, as well as how students will participate in classroom activities and lessons. Every aspect of the classroom should be taken into consideration to create the most vivid mental image possible.

The purpose of this exercise is twofold. First, it will help to remove a lot of the tension, stress, and anxiety associated with the first days of school and dealing with new or unfamiliar students. It will also serve as the catalyst for creating a plan for dealing with potentially difficult classroom behavioral situations. Mental visualization might sound a little weird at first, but trust me it works. So instead of being caught like a deer in headlights when a behavior problem occurs, the teacher will be able to react in a manner that is appropriate for the displayed behavior, exuding confidence and control.

After the positive mental image has been formed, then the teacher should ask him- or herself questions similar to the following:

- What is my teaching style? How can I convey that to students while appealing to their learning styles?
- What rules need to be in place to ensure that my positive mental image can become a reality?
- What do I need from students to ensure that I am able to deliver instruction effectively? How will my classroom rules coincide with the classroom activities associated with the daily lessons?
- What are the things that I absolutely will not tolerate in class (the nonnegotiable issues)? What are the issues on which I might be more flexible?
- If a student violates one or more of the classroom rules, how will I respond? How will I respond if a student verbally disrespects me?
- What are appropriate consequences that I can consistently administer in the classroom?
- What strategies or procedures can I use to maintain order and safety for all students in the classroom?
- How will I deal with major behavior problems? How will I deal with minor ones?
- What are misbehaviors that necessitate a referral to the administrator? Which are ones I can handle in the classroom?
- When should I attempt to contact parents? Which problems should I try to address solely with the student?

These questions are just some that urban teachers should consider before developing routines, norms, procedures, and common practices within the classroom. Once the teacher has established solid answers to these questions, he or she can begin to formulate those ideas in writing.

MAKE THE CLASSROOM CONDUCIVE FOR LEARNING

The next few pages are very important. Urban school teachers should follow the principles presented there to the letter, only deviating to fit the unique needs of a particular situation. This is where the rubber meets the road. In fact, you might want to refer to this chapter frequently until you have mastered all of the strategies outlined. Some strategies may seem common for all teachers (regardless of the setting), while some may seem outside the box. Nevertheless, all of the points mentioned should be followed by the urban school teacher in order to have a successfully managed classroom.

The first thing urban teachers must do is create an atmosphere conducive for learning. An atmosphere conducive to learning can be created by the manner in which the room is decorated as well as by the arrangement of the seats, furniture, and equipment. The classroom should be a visually stimulating place. When students walk into the classroom, they should instantly know it is a place of learning based on what they see.

Many teachers today underestimate the value of room décor, and they neglect to devote significant time to develop this area. This is a big mistake because many urban schools are housed in dilapidated buildings in desperate need of renovations. Also, many urban children live in projects and public housing that would be considered substandard for most middle-class Americans. Some of the older schools were even built from the same materials (bricks and mortar) used to build the neighborhood projects, so there is usually a striking resemblance between the appearance of some urban schools and the surrounding public housing.

In most urban communities there is very little home ownership, businesses, or solid investments in the community on behalf of its residents. Because of this, a culture develops among the residents of most poor urban communities in the United States that willfully devalues and neglects the communities in which they live. The problem is intensified when you mixed in all of the community's other ills (i.e., violence, drugs, gangs, high unemployment, mental illness, teen pregnancy, illiteracy, etc.), and it becomes easy to see why urban communities are dismal places to live. Why is this important to know and how does this relate to creating a classroom conducive to learning?

This connects to creating an atmosphere conducive to learning because urban students typically do not see many beautiful or stimulating types of natural scenery. Most students who live in such communities rarely go outside their particular neighborhoods. Urban communities are typically void of trees, grass, fresh smells, or beautiful scenery. The communities usually consist of condemned buildings, broken glass, graffiti, trash, and rubble. If urban students see drab settings in the community and see drab settings at school, the school will inevitably be treated the same way as the community (i.e., devalued, unappreciated, disrespected).

As I stated previously, the school is an extension of the community and not altogether a separate entity. If the culture of neglect and disregard for property is a permeable part of the community's culture, then it will also spill over into the school. According to Macciomei and Rubin (1999), behavior is a direct result of an environment. If the classroom environment is viewed and presented by the teacher as a place of learning and held in high regard, then the students will treat it as such. If the room is drab, dirty, and void of color and life, then the students will treat it the same way the projects and surrounding community are treated.

Urban teachers can combat this by making the classroom visually stimulating. Some of the things that add to a visually stimulating classroom are:

- Plants
- Unit themes
- Bulletin boards
- Flavorful scents
- Maps and charts
- Posted students' work
- Motivational quotes and sayings
- Content wall postings and hangings

- Pictures of prominent historical figures
- Posters of celebrities who positively endorse education.

This list is not exhaustive. Teachers should be as creative as possible when decorating their rooms and try to add their own personal touches. If the room needs painting, contact the school's administrators to see if you can put in a requisition to have the room painted. If that process doesn't work fast enough, ask if you can paint it yourself. You could even get some of the students to assist you and turn the activity into a beautification project or learning activity.

If your school doesn't have money in its budget for room decorations, then it would be wise for the teacher to use his or her own money and write it off during tax time. If you don't have the extra cash, then I suggest you borrow decorations from a colleague or beg for donations. Do whatever you have to in order to make the classroom as pleasant as possible. Be mindful not to go overboard. You do not have to cover every square inch of the room with something. The goal is to stimulate and beautify, not to crowd and clutter, which could have a reverse effect.

Teachers should also be mindful of their own dress and attire. The way one looks is often an indication of how one feels. Within my educational career, I've seen many teachers come to work dressed unprofessionally. When I say unprofessional, I'm referring to garments that are too revealing (exposing cleavage, back, or navel), sloppy (not pressed, torn, or soiled), or contain inappropriate logos or messages. Teachers must be mindful of the images they display in front of students. They are living examples to students of how professionals should dress and conduct themselves each day.

PROPERLY ARRANGE THE CLASSROOM FURNITURE

The next step would be to devote some attention to the seating and furniture arrangement. Proper arrangements of the classroom furniture and room décor go hand in hand. If arranged properly, the furniture will enhance the room, creating a more stimulating effect. Itcms that typically take up the most space in a classroom are the students' desks, the teacher's desk, book shelves, file cabinets, electronic equipment (computers, projectors, recorders, etc.), and storage closets.

With the exception of the electronic equipment and the students' desks, other items should be placed along the back walls or in corners where students frequent the least. You can even decorate them to camouflage their appearance. If you have no use for such items, or anything else for that matter, get rid of them. They will only take up space and detract from the atmosphere you're trying to create. The electronic equipment such as computers should have a designated area near electrical outlets, which is usually along a side wall. All other equipment should be stored and locked away until you need it.

Before setting up the room, there are some questions teachers should consider:

- How will students access classroom supplies?
- How should the students' desk be arranged?
- Where will students put unfinished or graded work?
- Where will I put textbooks and supplemental materials?
- How many students can this classroom hold comfortably?
- How will students be able to move and interact in the classroom?
- What learning centers or workstations will I have? In what part of the room should I place them?

Be mindful that the classroom should be arranged in a way that teachers, students, and visitors can move throughout the room freely, without bumping into things or one another. The designated areas in the room (workstations, computers, supply areas, etc.) should be labeled and visibly posted.

If applicable, there should also be rules and instructions posted on how to use the equipment and how to work in those areas. These rules should be reviewed with students before they attempt to work in the areas and should be referenced by the teacher frequently until the desired behavior is achieved. Students should not only be made aware of these key areas, but also how to use the tools available to them. This will establish and reinforce the expectations by providing clarity and removing all ambiguity.

The most important item of furniture is the students' desks. Many teachers, especially novice ones, do not take the time to arrange the desks properly, which can lead to increased classroom management problems. They simply put the desk in rows or create a seating chart from a pregenerated class roaster. Putting desks in rows makes it easy for custodians to do their jobs but not necessarily for teachers to do theirs. According to Jones (2007), the desks should be arranged to accommodate the type of instruction rendered. Classroom seating should be subject to the lesson being taught, which changes depending on the lesson.

For example, if a teacher gives the bulk of the instruction from a board located on the side wall, then the seats should be arranged so that students are directly facing the teacher (and the board), not the front of the room. I once observed a teacher who had such an issue. She arranged the desks so students faced the front of the room, but she delivered instruction from the board located on the side of the room. This seating arrangement caused students to face one way, and have to turn sideways in order to receive instruction. The awkward positioning caused students to strain their necks, which led them to turn to a more natural position. This slight adjustment caused students to lose focus, which led to off-task behavior and increased disruptions.

One final note about arranging students' desks: teachers should make sure they are able to clearly see every seat in the classroom. There are several discipline models that discuss the various ways to arrange a classroom. Teachers should select one that best meets the lesson they're delivering and the overall needs of the students.

DEVELOP YOUR CLASSROOM RITUALS

Once the room is transformed into a stimulating environment conducive to learning, the next step is to develop routines, norms, procedures, and practices (your rituals). Classroom routines are established to ensure that the classroom runs smoothly and efficiently (Burden, 2003). Common routines, practices, procedures, and norms are important elements of classroom management that urban teachers must vehemently work to establish and maintain. It is one of the reasons why I stated that urban teachers need to know what students' lives are like outside the school setting as well as have a keen understanding of the psychological, physical, and emotional needs of the students they serve.

Most urban students, especially those living in poverty, are accustomed to a life of uncertainty. One day they have plenty of food to eat, and the next day they don't. The utilities are on in their apartments one day, but disconnected the next. A loved one could be at home one day, and in jail the next. They could be living with their mother on Monday, but by Friday, they're living with their grandmother or relative without any advanced notice. One day they're laughing and conversing with a friend, the next day that friend has fallen victim to random violence in the neighborhood. The list goes on and on. The routines you establish will not only add to the fluidity of the class, but it will also give students a sense of security, consistency, stability, and normalcy that would be nonexistent in some cases.

Some of the most common routines and procedures are centered on the following areas:

- Late arrivals
- Labeling papers
- The start of class
- Taking attendance
- Dismissal from class
- The use of equipment
- Social behavioral norms
- Working in stations or groups
- Entering and exiting the room
- Signals to get students attention
- Emergency drills and procedures

- Finishing assignments early
- Students moving around the room
- Makeup work and grading policies
- Collection and distribution of papers or materials
- Going to the restroom and other places.

It is important to note that the rituals you establish must be explained clearly to the students. Don't assume students will automatically know what to do or properly interpret what the expectations are on their own. I recommend the bulk of the time spent with students during the first few days of school be strictly devoted to establishing, reviewing, and practicing routines. Discuss the rationale behind the routines and their importance.

Make sure they understand the routine by providing clarity through modeling and giving students opportunities to practice. You want to imbed the routines in their heads so they become second nature to them. One final note on routines: Depending on the situation or activity done in class, the teacher might have to establish a new routine or procedure to fit that particular situation. If this happens, the teacher must be flexible enough to make adjustments and work to establish the new procedure in a manner consistent with more common ones.

CLASSROOM RULES AND CONSEQUENCES

After formalizing the routines and procedures, urban school teachers must develop rules and consequences for students. This is another vital part of a successfully managed classroom. Before developing the rules and consequences, you must take into consideration the information outlined in the previous chapters. Think about some of the issues that students have in their home environments and how this translates into behaviors at school.

Factors in students' lives should be taken under consideration, but they should not be used as an excuse to lower the expectations for proper student behavior. Without a certain level of proper behavior on behalf of students, no learning will take place in the classroom. Think back to how you envisioned your classroom and how you wanted it to operate. Remember your nonnegotiables? Now use that positive mental image as the focal point for designing your classroom rules. According to Kaiser and Rasminsky (2007), teachers should establish three to six rules to govern the classroom. It should not be an exhaustive list of "thou shall nots," but a short list of rules that teachers feel are important for the overall well-being of the classroom and everyone in it.

The most powerful approach to forming classroom rules is to get the students' input when developing them. Giving students a say in the rules that will affect them is the most strategic way for teachers to gain students' acceptance of the rules. This method signals to students that the teacher values their opinions and the things they have to say. It also creates a sense of oneness in the class, forming ties and relationships that lead to rapport building.

The teacher could write two or three rules and have the students write the rest, or the teacher could choose to collaborate with students to create all of the rules. When I was a high school teacher, I employed both tactics to create classroom rules. After soliciting students' opinions, I found out why they felt the rules they came up with were important to them.

When finalized, I wrote the rules on poster board and posted them in various places in the room where students could readily see them. Whether the teacher designs all the rules alone or in collaboration with the students, the rules should be posted and visible to everyone. They should also be clear and free of ambiguous language and negative overtones. For example, it is improper to state a classroom rule as, "No profanity or bad language will be used in the classroom." I say this because the rule starts off with the word "No," which has a negative overtone. Second, "profanity" and "bad language" could be subjective. There are some profane words that are universally recognized, but some are not. I've known teachers that considered the word "crap" as bad language, but many students in urban communities might not consider that a harsh word. A proper way to state the rule could be, "Students will use appropriate language and treat everyone with respect."

Just like with the classroom rules, the consequences for breaking a rule should also be clearly understood by all students, free of ambiguous language, and posted in the classroom. Student collaboration should also be encouraged by the teacher for this aspect as well. Consequences should be progressive by design, leading to different stages of discipline. The teacher should attempt to handle student discipline issues in varying degrees before sending the student out of class with a referral. The following is an example of possible progressive consequences:

- Verbal warning: First offense
- Parental contact or student-centered action: Second offense
- Detention or alternate student-centered action: Third offense
- Student and/or parent conference: Fourth offense
- Written behavioral contract: Fifth offense
- Referral to the administrator: Sixth offense
- Restart the process after the administrative referral.

When designing your consequences, make sure they are flexible and that you are able to actually enforce them. If you notice in my example, as part of the second and third violations I have the words "or student-centered action." This gives the teacher some flexibility, which can be used as a leverage point with students.

For example, I once had a student who had an issue with leaving trash on the classroom floor, and he often left his workspace dirty. After the verbal warning, I told the student that if he didn't clean up his area properly, I would either call his mother or make him clean up the entire classroom (hence the student action). Some students dread having their parents called, especially for something trivial.

The student elected to stop the negative behavior out of fear of a possible call home. This also gave me an opportunity to develop rapport with the student. While cleaning up the classroom with him, I was not only able to reinforce the expectations, but I was also able to find out more about the student—his interests, beliefs, and ideas about school. I was able to bond with the student in a more meaningful way, which led to the student self-correcting his behavior.

Teachers should be flexible and progressive with their consequences because it is important to never run out of options or go from moderate to a state of emergency over a menial offense. For example, Mike is in the fifth grade. It's 9:00 a.m. and he is off task and "playing the dozens" with his friends in the back of the classroom. Ms. Walker, his teacher, notices his behavior and says, "If you don't stop, I'm going to call your mother and you will not be allowed to go on the field trip."

Mike momentarily stops his behavior before repeating it moments later. The teacher stops instructing the class and calls Mike's mother on her cell phone. Ms. Walker briefly explains the situation to his parent and then hands Mike the cell phone. While the teacher resumes teaching, everyone in the classroom can hear Mike's mother yelling and cursing on the phone, threatening to "beat his butt" when he gets home. Ms. Walker also informs Mike that he can't go on the field trip. It is now 9:45 a.m., Mike is not going on the field trip and he's going to face an angry mother when he gets home later. Will this stop Mike's misbehaviors for the rest of the day? Probably not, because in a fifth grader's mind, he's probably saying to himself, "Why should I behave? What more could she do to me? I'm already in trouble."

He will probably interpret Ms. Walker's actions as unfair compared to his actions, and continue to misbehave for the entire day, which could eventually lead to Mike being sent out of class. Teachers should not "empty the bank" too soon. They should move progressively through levels of consequences, making sure students are aware every step of the way. Also, when enforcing the rules and consequences, the teacher must exercise fairness and consistency.

Fairness and *consistency* are two words that can't be stressed enough. If students sense that the teacher's rules apply to some students and not others, then the teacher's credibility will be lost. Even if one of the "good students" violates a rule, the teacher should handle it with the same zeal as with a student who causes disruptions on a regular basis. This will send a message to all the students that the teacher is fair and treats everyone the same (in regards to discipline).

Urban teachers must say what they mean, and mean what they say. To piggyback off the previous example, the student who doesn't clean his workspace might plead with you not to call his mother in exchange for cleaning up the entire classroom, or serving a detention as a consequence, only to repeat the same negative behavior again tomorrow. This is part of the test. The student is trying to figure out how far he is able to go before the teacher will actually call his mother, or if he can beguile the teacher into not calling by saying sorry or vowing to change after a rule is violated. When this happens the teacher has to show the student that he or she means business. If you say you're going to call home after giving the student the opportunity to change on his or her own, then make the call. Don't be tricked by false promises of future compliance, because if the student was going to comply, he or she would have done it after being given the verbal warning(s).

A final note about rules and consequences: they are necessary to provide structure, organization, and order. Many urban students are missing such components in their lives. Even though they might initially resist, they want someone to correct and discipline them. They want someone to be consistent. Deep down inside, they want people to care enough not to let them run amuck. The rules and consequences should be established on the first day of school. They should be reviewed, modeled, and revisited for at least the first two to four weeks and then periodically throughout the school year. This will firmly cement the expectations, which will decrease the types and amount of issues the teacher will have in the future.

DEALING WITH MISBEHAVIORS

Just because you designed a set of rules and consequences and reviewed them with your students doesn't mean you're going to get total compliance. Designing the rules is the easy part, but gaining full compliance is where the real work must be done. This is the part that separates the strong urban teachers from the weak. Be certain that there will be some resistance from students. Urban school teachers should expect resistance from students on all fronts.

Within most middle-class and affluent environments, people generally attain authority, respect, and power based on their credentials (years of experiences, task accomplished, level of education, etc.) or position (CEO, manager, principal, teacher, etc.). This notion of attaining authority and respect is the exact opposite for people who live in poor urban communities. People gain respect based on their actions.

A person who has any level of respect in urban communities attained it only after having been tested in some manner. It doesn't matter if you're talking about the best boxer, basketball player, drug dealer, pimp, hustler, or dancer. There is an intensely competitive nature within low socioeconomic communities because everyone is fighting for the limited resources available to them. No one gets respect simply because of a title or position. Respect is based on showing and proving.

UNDERSTANDING STUDENT RESISTANCE

Many urban school teachers find it hard to get respect from their students because they assume that simply because they've been given the title of teacher, and the responsibilities thereof, students will automatically give them respect and authority over the classroom. Teachers should view misbehavior from students as simply part of a game, or just another aspect of the urban teaching landscape. It is an environmental trait students have learned over time, which also transfers over into the classroom environment. With that being said, I'd like to let you in on a little secret. Resistance from students is the best indicator to inform teachers when they are gaining ground with them.

For example, take an individual living in a poor urban neighborhood who wants to play basketball. He will not get the attention of older or more established players in the neighborhood until he starts to elevate his skills. Once the playing skills have risen to a certain level, a buzz will go out through the neighborhood. This is the point when the real competition starts. Other players will challenge him in a variety of ways.

They will talk trash, play roughly, use intimidation, try to plant seeds of doubt in his head, or use any other tactic to gain an advantage. It's like putting the player through a test or rites of passage. If the player is able to withstand the test by winning despite the obstacles, or continue to play at a high level while in a hostile environment, then the tests will cease and the player under scrutiny will get respect from the very same people who once doubted him.

In order to successfully manage an urban classroom, the teacher must operate from a certain mindset. First, he or she can't take things personal. There is a common phrase that's used in the business world that states, "It's business, never personal." Urban school teachers should adopt this phrase as a motto for dealing with students' behavioral issues.

Don't take the push back, resistance, or backlash from students personal. The moment teachers start taking resistance from students as a personal affront to their teaching abilities, two things usually occur. They either develop an adversarial stance toward students or they withdraw completely, which could adversely affect their feelings of efficacy. If urban school teachers are not able to perform amid the resistance, they will not earn the students' respect and the misbehavior will continue.

Let's walk in the shoes of the average urban student who lives in poverty. This student is deprived in one or more of his or her physical, psychological, emotional, or social needs. There may be some feelings of neglect, abandonment, hopelessness, or some combination of these. At some point in the urban student's life, he or she has acquired some of the negative environmental traits of the community and other tactics for survival.

This same student reports to school and finds a visually stimulating classroom (if you followed the suggestions earlier in this chapter), which is a direct contrast from what he or she normally sees in the community environment on a daily basis. There is a teacher who is always smiling and cheerful when greeting students every day and is always encouraging by saying positive things to students, which is a contrast from the derogatory language common in the neighborhood. The student could have heard positive things about the teacher from other students, or he or she could have sensed the teacher's passion and zeal for educating students. The student also notices how the teacher is constantly working to establish oneness, fairness, and consistency within the classroom (even though the student may not use those same words to articulate or express him- or herself).

At this point the teacher has caused a dichotomy in the student's mind. On one level the student is thinking to him- or herself, "I like this teacher. This teacher seems like a nice person. I might learn a lot in this class. I might like this class. I might even get a good grade." As soon as the positive thoughts fill the student's mind, in comes the negative thinking that exists from the many years of being deprived and exposed to adverse cultural and environmental influences. "This isn't real. I not going to pass. I'm going to fail. This teacher don't really like me. This teacher is no different from anyone else. What is this teacher up to? I'm not smart enough. I'll probably get in trouble again."

Because this dualism exist in the student's mind, he or she will then have to find out if the teacher's motives are sincere. The student will begin to test the waters with the teacher by gradually undermining the rules or acting out to get attention. Since the student only knows how to communicate in ways that are acceptable for survival in his or her neighborhood, it would be safe to say the teacher will misread most of the student's actions (especially if the teacher doesn't understand the cultural environment of the student). The student's perceived negative behaviors will escalate, and the student will be viewed by the teacher as being disrespectful and uncooperative (just to name a few).

For the sake of this example, let's say the teacher hasn't read this book or learned any of the tools I outlined in the previous chapters. Eventually, one of two things will happen: the teacher will either lose control of the classroom and fail miserably or there will be a frequent exchange of students displaying negative behaviors (which the teacher doesn't understand) and the teacher will end up sending students out of class to the principal's office. When this happens, it reinforces the student's negative opinions about the school, its staff, and the student's place within the school. This is a common scenario in many urban classrooms throughout the country.

As I stated previously, the dichotomy that is formed in the student's head and the resistance teachers receive are, in most cases, an indication that the teacher is making positive strides in the right direction. The harder the resistance from students, the more potential for positive influence. Most teachers who experience resistance from students when trying to gain compliance to classroom rules will misinterpret resistance as a personal attack and think the students do not like them or the subject being taught. Some even go as far as to label the student as being bad, at-risk, unreachable, or attempt to get the student out of the classroom or suspended from school.

In addition to serving as a test for the teacher, the resistance displayed by students is nothing more than a manifestation of the students' deficiencies. It is a defense mechanism some students have developed to avoid getting their feelings hurt or being embarrassed or ashamed; while at the same time, it serves as their official calling card for help. Urban teachers must understand this in order to properly manage their classrooms and provided the educational support urban students need and deserve.

When students misbehave, they're testing their teachers to see exactly what they are made of. They want to find out if the teachers are going to be there for the long haul, or if the teacher is going to bail on them like so many other adults in their lives. They don't want to be set up for another let down. They don't want to get attached to another person who's not going to be there. And above all else, they don't want to begin to care for someone who's going to eventually hurt them. This is one of the key reasons for the resistance. If urban educators want to really get a hold on classroom management, then they must look at it from this perspective.

It is at the point of resistance where some urban teachers throw in the towel. They become fearful of any potential conflicts from students, making them ineffective at maintaining order. In contrast, teachers should meet resistance head on with a befitting consequence. I liken this interaction to a fisherman who catches a big fish on his fishing line. The fish will resist by tugging, pulling, and jerking. Some fish will also try to jump out of the water in an effort to free themselves from the line. If the fisherman wants to catch the fish, he has to withstand the resistance by holding on to the line, pulling back, and reeling the fish in.

Likewise with misbehaving students, when teachers experience resistance from students, they should stand their ground and dig the hook deeper and totally win the students over. Be careful: students' resistance could manifest itself in a variety of ways. It could start off with subtle things like ignoring basic directions from the teacher and simple class rules, and then progress to excessive tardiness or absences, loud talking, aggressive gestures and movements, profanity, even throwing furniture and slamming doors. Remember, the teacher can't look at the outward appearance and emotion. The student's outward appearance is typically the manner in which he or she is trying to disguise his or her true feelings.

THE THREE CATEGORIES OF URBAN STUDENTS

Throughout my years of experience, educational study, and dialogue with other educators across the country, I've determined that most urban students fall into one of three categories: (1) Passive Resisters, (2) Average Joes, and (3) Extreme Supremes. Each type has a distinctive set of behaviors that teachers should understand when trying to deal with students' behavioral issues.

First, there is the Passive Resister. The Passive Resister is a student who is usually nonaggressive and quiet to the point where he or she could easily go unnoticed in the classroom. I call them Passive Resisters because they resist instruction and disregard following rules in nonaggressive, subtle ways. They are almost always respectful and polite, but they will fall off task academically.

For example, they will sit in class and look as if they're paying attention, but not take any notes or follow along with the teacher. In a group setting, they will physically be part of the group, but not do their portion of the group's assignment. Their minds will be somewhere else for the entire class period. In some of the more severe cases, these students will choose not to respond to basic directions or will rarely speak to the teacher or others in class.

Students who fit into this category may be lacking in several of their psychological, emotional, physical, and social needs. This type of student will not volunteer to answer questions or read aloud in front of others. They have a tendency to internalize things that happen to them and rarely show emotions, so it's hard to read them. If this kind of student is not engaged in the learning, he or she could cut class or stop coming altogether as opposed to complaining or telling someone about his or her problems.

The best way to deal with Passive Resisters is to constantly monitor their activity. Teachers need to move around the room, call on them to answer questions, and reinforce the task they need to do within the class period. The teacher could also give these students roles and duties within the classroom to make them feel more involved. For example, they could be responsible for sharpening pencils, passing out graded papers, or cleaning the boards. The goal with these students is to keep them engaged, interested, and participating. The teacher's work around creating oneness and establishing rapport in the class will be enough to keep the Passive Resisters on the right track. In a class of twenty, an urban teacher can expect to see three to five students of this type.

Next, there is the Average Joe. This is the largest group in any given urban classroom. In a classroom of twenty, six to eighteen could be classified in this group. These students may be lacking in one or more of their needs, but the deficiency is not significant. For example, these students might come from a single parent home, but the one parent they do have is going above and beyond the call of duty to fulfill the students needs or is getting help from extended family. The ability levels of Average Joe's vary, but collectively, they are capable of digesting the learning materials and producing good work.

The most notable characteristic about students in this group is that they have a strong need to fit in and be like the majority. They don't want to stand out too far from the pack. If there is a popular tennis shoe that the majority of students are wearing, then the Average Joe wants a pair as well. If there is a popular movie star everyone is talking about, then the Average Joe wants to be in on the conversation. If the majority of the students are getting good grades, then the Average Joe will also.

A teacher's inability to handle this group of students could have great implications on classroom management. The majority of a teacher's efforts (instructionally and behaviorally) should be geared for this group because they are the largest segment of the classroom population. Successfully reaching this group will catapult the entire class to new academic heights.

The last category is the Extreme Supreme. In a class of twenty, the urban teacher can expect to see one to three students who fall into this group. These students usually have low-ability levels, but in some cases, they can be very bright. I call these students Extreme Supreme because they have multiple high-level deficiencies, regardless of their intelligence.

They can be very sensitive, emotional, and have a tendency to overreact to even the most trivial situations. They will also exhibit behaviors such as using profanity toward students and staff, constant attention seeking, refusal to follow simple directions, cutting classes, fighting with peers, and rejecting authority.

The attitudes will be so bad, and the language so foul, it would make the teacher wish the students would disappear and never return. They will also be the ones who will have the power to captivate the other students' attention. The Average Joe and Passive Resister will be in awe of the Extreme Supreme in the same way that audiences are captivated by so-called reality television shows. It's like a dramatic soap opera unfolding right before their eyes. Seeing a peer act foolishly in class is very entertaining to most students.

If the Extreme Supreme is able to dominate the class so that the norm is chaos, confusion, and disorganization, then the Average Joe will follow the norm and start acting up as well. Remember, the Average Joe just wants to be associated with the larger group. Likewise, if the norm is positive and one that fosters learning, then the Average Joe's will follow suit. If left alone, the Extreme Supreme students will wreak havoc, making it almost impossible for the teacher to recover. These students should not be left alone. They are the ones who are in need of the most help. The teachers who fail to respond appropriately to these students are usually the ones who have the worst classroom management skills.

Dealing with these types of students is crucial because not only should teachers attempt to reach such students and build a connection, but the manner in which it is done will also have an impact on the other students in the class. Remember, the students who act out the most are the ones who have the other students' attention. If the student with the severe behavioral issues is allowed to cause problems in class and get away with it, then the other students who admire this student will do the same. But if the student with the severe behavioral issues is dealt with effectively by the teacher, it will send out an equally powerful message to the other students. They'll know that misbehavior in class is not acceptable.

STRATEGIC ACTION

The assertive proactive teacher will be able to deter many of the minor problems from the majority of students by using the strategies outlined in this book, but it takes some skill to deal with the Extreme Supreme student. When the Extreme Supreme student goes on the attack, he or she will usually direct the aggression at the teacher. This is done to maintain the status with the rest of the students who are watching and to test the limits with the classroom teacher. Again, do not take it as a personal attack. Think of it as a power move for control of the class. The teacher has to move swiftly and strategically because the other students are watching to see how the teacher will react as well. The teacher's actions will dictate how other students will respond behaviorally in the future.

There is an old saying that goes, "Strike the shepherd and the sheep will scatter." This means that if you attack and defeat the leader, then the ones following the leader will start running. The "sheep" will run because they have no direction, and leadership that the "shepherd" used to provide is now obsolete. The scattered sheep will ultimately surrender to the next person who shows him- or herself as a dominate figure.

The same holds true for most students in urban school classrooms, regardless of the age or grade of the students. The classroom teacher must handle the Extreme Supreme student swiftly and firmly. The classroom teacher should be the dominant figure in the classroom. There should be no doubt in anyone's mind who is in charge. Students need to be under the influence of the classroom teacher and not the influence of a student who is showing off or misbehaving.

If the teacher successfully handles the Extreme Supreme, then the rest will be a piece of cake. This is true because in the average student's minds, if the teacher can deal with the one whom they admire and consider to be "tough," then surely the teacher will be able to deal with them just as easily. They will adhere to the classroom rules with minimal resistance.

Now, I know what you're probably thinking at this point. You're wondering how to prevent the Extreme Supreme students from turning the classroom upside down. In order for the classroom teacher to get the students in this group to comply with the classroom rules, and actively learning, the teacher and Extreme Supremes will engage in a series of exchanges. It can be compared to a chess match, with each moving and countering.

The exchanges between the teacher and Extreme Supreme can happen at different times within the school year, but the sooner the better. The teacher needs to establish his or her presence early so the rest of the school year can follow smoothly. The exchanges between the teacher and student will usually follow a certain sequence of events, but if each is handled correctly, the teacher will be able to drastically reduce or totally eliminate the undesirable behaviors being displayed by the student.

The first thing that the teacher will notice from the Extreme Supreme is minor misbehaviors that occur frequently. The teacher may notice similar actions from other students, so identifying the Extreme Supreme might be a little tricky at first. The students in this group will eventually stand out (through their noncompliance) after the teacher has gone through the rules and consequences. Students in the other two groups will initially comply after one or two verbal warnings or after the teacher has assigned a consequence that is aligned to a particular action.

The Extreme Supreme will continue to display the behavior despite the teacher's warnings or consequences. The Extreme Supreme will also display the minor misbehaviors at a higher rate than the other students. The minor behaviors could include, but are not limited to, chronic tardiness, random loud outbursts in class, distracting others, eating and drinking in class, failure to follow simple directions, failure to follow simple directions, nonparticipation, or refusing to do any work.

To combat these minor behaviors, the teacher must respond quickly, as soon as the student displays the negative behaviors (strike the shepherd), in order to send the message that constant disruptions will not be allowed. Some teachers make the mistake of ignoring the misbehavior(s) in hopes that it will go away, but it never does. The student will get progressively worse if the teacher doesn't act swiftly.

Swift action can come in many forms. Depending on the behavior, the teacher may decided to verbally reinforce the expectations for positive behavior, change the student's seating arrangement, pull the student aside for a brief conference, or make parental contact. The goal at this stage is for the teacher to maintain his or her composure. You want to let the Extreme Supreme, and the other students, know that you're serious about maintaining order and a positive learning environment.

The next stage is when the real fun starts. This is the stage in which the student will become irritated. The swift action on the teacher's behave for minor misbehaviors is going to cause discomfort with the student because the student wasn't able to do what he or she is accustom to doing (causing confusion in class) and because the teacher didn't respond as predicted (ignoring the student/putting the student out). Unfortunately, the Extreme Supreme has been allowed to display inappropriate behaviors in class throughout his or her schooling without much intervention from prior teachers or from responsible adults. It's almost like the student has been conditioned to believe that certain behaviors will elicit certain responses from teachers.

Historically, when an Extreme Supreme frequently displays certain minor behaviors, he or she receives positive affirmation from the students while the teacher does nothing to stop it. When the teacher doesn't respond as the student predicts or curtails the level of affirmation received from the other students in class, the student will become irritated and agitated. It is at this point when the Extreme Supreme will turn the pressure up a level or two. The next level from the Extreme Supreme will come in the form of verbal disrespect toward the teacher.

This is the point where 80 to 90 percent of urban school teachers wither away. This is usually where they throw in the towel because they can't deal with this level of resistance from their students. In contrast, this is the point when the teacher should smile. The verbal disrespect is usually the Extreme Supreme's final attempt to get his or her way. The student has learned that if he or she shows this side of behavior, it results in the affirmation he or she was trying to achieve. When students display this side of their behavior, the teacher should become a little excited because the students are running out of ammunition.

When students resort to verbally disrespecting the teacher, they don't have anything else left. Verbally disrespecting the teacher is their ace in the whole—their trump card. These students' past school experiences have led them to believe that when they use a little profanity, the teacher will either kick them out of class or back down and allow them to change the environment of the class. Again, teachers should not take the verbal disrespect personal. It's the student's last attempt at a power move to disrupt the class and gain, or maintain, the adoration of his or her peers. This may be harder for some teachers than others, but when this kind of behavior is displayed, teachers need to dig deep and gather all the intestinal fortitude they are able to muster in order to weather the storm. Remember, after every rain storm, there is always sunshine.

The student(s) might also display behaviors such as violating your space (intimidation), displaying inappropriate hand gestures (pointing and waving), using profane terminology and derogatory names, slamming doors, knocking things over, or making threats. This level of disrespect will be almost entirely aimed at the teacher. The teacher must attack the misbehavior by reinforcing the expectations and desired behavior, followed by a consequence among alternatives.

For example, when I was a classroom teacher, I had an Extreme Supreme explode on me because I didn't allow him to sleep in class. He put his head down on three separate occasions, two of which I had given him verbal warnings. On the third time, I noticed he had fallen completely asleep. So I politely tapped his shoulder and suggested that he go into the hall to get a drink of water to help him wake up. He responded by shouting, "Get yo damn hands off me and leave me alone!" I responded by saying, "Listen (student's name), you will not speak to me in that way again. I want the same respect that I give you in return. Now you can either sit up and participate with your classmates, or you can contact your mother to see how she feels about your behavior."

In my example, I tackled the undesirable behavior (head down/ disrespect), reinforced the desirable behavior (sit up and participate/speak to the teacher appropriately), and followed with a consequence among alternatives (participate with the class/call the students mother). Depending on how severe the level of behavior being displayed, the teacher may elect to not give an alternative consequence. Some behaviors are so severe that the student must be removed from the class quickly in order to preserve the learning environment for the other students.

In the scenario above, the student continued to use more profanity toward me and would not comply to my request for him to
start working. The school's security had to escort him out of the
classroom. This is typical Extreme Supreme behavior. When given
a consequence among alternatives, the Extreme Supreme will normally elect the choice that is most defiant. This is just part of the
game. This is done because the student has an audience (his or her
peers in class) so the student wants to keep up the image his or
her peers have grown to respect and admire. When this happens,
removing the Extreme Supreme from his or her peers in class is the
best action to take.

APPLYING CORRECTIVE ACTION

This brings us to the next stage, which is the corrective action process.
This is the follow-up after the extreme behavior has been displayed.
This is a very important part that many teachers tend to neglect
when sending a student out of the classroom. When some teachers
send a student out of the classroom, they believe that they've gained
a victory because the student was temporarily removed from the
classroom or possibly suspended. In reality the teacher hasn't really accomplished anything. Yes, the student was sent out of class,
or maybe even disciplined by the principal, but when the student
returns to class, the negative behavior will start all over again. This
happens to most urban school teachers because they fail to apply
corrective action after the student has been sent out.

In order for corrective action to be effective, the classroom
teacher must be part of the disciplinary or corrective process. Since
the situation started with the classroom teacher, it's only right that
the situation end with the teacher as well. In order to provide corrective action, the teacher (and administrator overseeing the discipline at the school) should isolate the student from his or her peers,
preferably in an office, conference room, or place where students do
not frequently visit. This will take away the audience and remove
the student's desire to show off.

In isolation the student will be more likely to listen to what the teacher or administrator has to say. This is also when you'll see the real nature of the student and not some image he or she is trying to uphold. The teacher should use this time to ask some questions:

- Why did you go off like that?
- Is there something else you want to talk about?
- What can I do to help you adjust better in class?
- How could you have handled the situation differently?
- What should you do next time if you're ever in a similar situation?
- Did something happen before class, or at home, that you want to talk about?
- How would your parents feel if they knew how you were behaving in class?
- If you were in the teacher's shoes, how would you have handled a student who behaved in the manner you did?

While discussing the situation with the student, the teacher's demeanor should be cool, calm, and collected. Even though the teacher is speaking about a very severe situation that happened in his or her classroom, the teacher's demeanor should not reflect it. This will show the student that you are unmoved by his or her previous antics.

Many teachers will make the mistake of using an isolated time with the student and principal as a means of firing back at the student. Since the teacher is in the room with another adult, the teacher feels a little more confident and bold. This is a very big mistake. The goal here is to change the behavior, not to get revenge.

Trying to get back at the student now will only complicate matters and promote the same behaviors when the student returns to class. While in such meetings, teachers should be firm, yet consolatory. They should be stern, yet empathetic. While speaking, the teacher should look the student directly in the eyes and speak using clear, confident, and concise language. The teacher should view this meeting as a turning point with the student, and it should be handled with care.

During this meeting, pay extra attention to the student's demeanor. He or she will be unsure of how to act because, for one, the student knows he or she was wrong; and two, because he or she may feel a little uncomfortable. Without the peers watching, the becomes like a fish out of water. Teachers should take their time and not let the student dictate the pace. Because the isolated setting is going to be uncomfortable for the student, he or she will want to get out of the meeting as quickly as possible, becoming more antsy with each passing minute.

Slow down and recap the situation and get the student to verbalize what was on his or her mind at the time and state the causes for his or her actions. Typical behaviors you may see from a student in such a meeting are long pauses between answers to questions, staring at the floor or looking away from the person talking, stuttering or muttered sentences, refusal to answer questions, or an emotional breakdown.

The emotional breakdown is usually caused by questions similar to the ones listed above. They are the type of questions that get to the root of the student's issue. During an emotional breakdown, it is not unusual to see students cry or open up about nonschool-related issues. In this state, the student will begin to share issues in his or her home life and environment, situations involving parents and relatives, problems in school, troubles with peers, or past or present abuses experienced.

When a student has an emotional breakdown, it is good for several reasons. First, the student was given a rare opportunity to release emotions that he or she had been carrying for a long time. The student was allowed to openly display his or her feelings without fear of being ridiculed or teased. It can be compared to an emotional cleansing.

All of the antics in class while in front of his or her peers were not indicative of the real character of the student. It was a false image manufactured to avoid embarrassment, pain, or to gain some form of acceptance. Urban educators need to understand this simple premise when encountering student misbehaviors. Don't look at the exterior because it's usually the opposite of the real nature of the student.

Second, the teacher is able to truly find out what's happening with the student. Many times the misbehavior isn't caused by anything associated with the student's home life or environment. The misbehavior is usually caused by an academic deficiency, not because the child is bad or has a terrible home life. The student usually misbehaves because he or she is trying to cover up deficiencies in reading, math, writing, speaking, or some other weakness. The isolated meetings allow the teacher to gain such valuable information. Once the teacher gains knowledge of the student's academic deficiency, the teacher can then strategically work to bring the student up to proficient levels, therefore eliminating the student's need to act out and disrupt the class.

Lastly, the student's emotional display will strengthen the bond between the student and teacher. Emotional settings and circumstances have a way of bonding people. The visceral experience from this type of meeting will lend itself to the teacher forming a tighter bond with the student, therefore strengthening the rapport. The student will realize that the teacher truly cares about his or her well-being.

The student will see the teacher as a supporter instead of a foe. Caution: When students have an emotional release, it might be a good idea to involve a counselor or the school's psychologist and to document the student's comments, depending on the nature of the conversation. This will give the school officials involved added protection and increase the chances that the student's issue will be resolved in the best manner possible.

The most critical piece in this process is the consequence the student receives. This final element cannot be left out. In the world outside of school, there are consequences for our actions. For example, what if that same student were to use profane language or threaten a police officer? How about the supervisor at his or her place of employment? What do you think would be the consequences? Jail? Loss of job? School prepares students for the real world in many ways.

Now, you could have the student suspended for the offense, but is that the goal you're after? My suggestion is to review the student code of conduct with the student so he or she knows what the consequences are for similar behavior displayed in the future. I would also suggest that the student be given a choice of consequences among alternatives as opposed to being suspended (on the first offense of course).

Giving the student a say in how he or she will be disciplined will foster a deeper level of compliance. The student will be more willing to agree to the consequence, and the teacher will also be able to build deeper connections with the student. The only time when I wouldn't allow the student a choice among disciplinary alternatives is after multiple violations of the same offense.

A few final points before concluding this chapter: First when dealing with student behavioral issues, the teacher must make a strong connection with the parents or some concerned adult. This connection must start early in the school year and must be an ongoing process. Parental involvement is very important to the corrective process of students' behavior. When and how you decided to inform parents during the corrective process is totally up to you as a professional and the rapport you've been able to establish with the parents previously. I'll discuss more on this subject in the next chapter.

Second, if you have encountered a student whose behavior is more extreme than normal and his or her academic ability is far lower than the other students, then the student might be a candidate for special education services. I'm not an advocate of thrusting students under the special education umbrella. Urban students, especially African American males, are disproportionately labeled with a special education handicap compared to their white (urban and nonurban) student counterparts. Many teachers who haven't attempted to understand the issues pertaining to the average urban school student make poor decisions and place undeserving labels on children.

I think a referral for special education services should only be considered as an option in the most severe cases. A teacher can identify the most severe cases based on a certain criteria. The majority of urban students will comply based on the teacher's organization, routines, norms, fairness, consistency, and relentless passion for education. You'll have a much smaller group of students who will comply after parents are contacted or consequences are assigned. The severe behavioral students, which comprise an even smaller group, will comply after you've had an isolated meeting with them (with the parents and another school official in attendance) and you've created a strategic plan targeting the student's academic deficiencies.

After the isolated meetings have occurred, there will be the one or two very extreme students who will not comply after you've gone through all of the above tactics multiple times; these are the students who will need special education services. I only recommend making this kind of referral for a student after the teacher has exhausted every avenue possible and the behavior hasn't changed. In this case, special education services might be exactly what the student needs in order to be successful in school. You could encounter one student of this nature every two to three years, therefore making special education services a viable option for the student's well-being; not as a dumping ground for students whom the teacher has trouble dealing with.

Finally, there have been a lot of things written in the media about school violence in the form of shootings, stabbings, and so forth. The fact of the matter is that violence against teachers happens rarely. The media sensationalize school violence in order to sell papers or to boost ratings. This sensationalized view also sparks fear and is one of the reasons why potentially qualified individuals opt to avoid teaching in urban schools.

As I stated previously, profanity or verbal disrespect and non-compliance to classroom rules are typically the worst urban school teachers experience from students. With that being said, if a teacher is ever in a situation where he or she feels unsafe with a student or a student threatens to do the teacher bodily harm, the teacher should not only have the student removed from his or her class but should also press charges. Teachers should never be subjected to work in an unsafe environment, nor should they put up with physical threats from students.

Early in my teaching career, I was teaching a class with my classroom door open. A male student, whom I didn't know, walked into my room, sat down in a chair, and began to talk to some of the students in my classroom. I asked the student to leave, but he didn't comply. After I persisted, the student begged me to let him stay until the bell rang for dismissal. I didn't honor his request and told him to leave immediately or I would call for security. Suddenly, the young man got out of the chair, walked in my face, and shouted, "F___ you! That's why I'm gonna shoot yo ass when you leave the buildin'!"

After making the threat, the student ran out of the classroom. I was totally shocked to say the least. I didn't understand how the student went from begging me to stay in my class one moment to threatening to shoot me the next without provocation. The student's reaction moved past profanity and disrespect. He actually made a threat on my life.

The end result was that the student was expelled from school for forty-five days and spent three months in a juvenile detention center. Before the expulsion, he tried to say he was sorry to avoid the punishment and stated that he didn't mean it. The student probably wasn't going to shoot me, but how was I to know? If he was brave enough to say it, he might try to make good on his promise. The young man had to learn that one can't go around making threats of that magnitude and expect to get away with it. That's not how the real world works. He had to learn that kind of behavior is not acceptable at school or anywhere in a rational society. Any student who makes a threat to do a teacher bodily harm should be prosecuted to the fullest extent of the law. It just might be the antidote for preventing the student from actually doing something extremely violent to someone else in the future.

CHAPTER SUMMARY POINTS

- Teacher should create an environment conducive to learning.
- It is important to establish rules, consequences, and norms in the classroom.
- Act swiftly and fairly when delivering student discipline.

- Teachers must be part of the corrective process of student discipline.
- Teachers shouldn't view resistance from students as a personal attack.
- There are three types of students: Passive Resisters, Average Joes, and Extreme Supremes.
- Teachers should know when to involve parents and administrators in the discipline process.

5

ESTABLISHING CONNECTIONS WITH PARENTS OR SOME CARING ADULT

One of the most important tasks you must accomplish as a teacher in an urban school is to form a solid connection with your students' parents. A teacher's ability to establish a working relationship with parents or guardians, will improve classroom management and reduce student behavioral issues significantly. It is almost unrealistic to expect long-lasting or permanent changes in students' behavior without parental involvement, but doing so is easier said than done.

Parents of urban school-aged children can be very elusive when it comes to teachers trying to establish rapport with them. Phone numbers and addresses change frequently. Also, students may not live with their biological parent(s), even though the student's official record might say otherwise. Many urban school-aged students are being raised by grandparents (usually the paternal grandmother), and in some cases they're living in foster or group homes. Also, it is not uncommon to find students living with multiple relatives during different points within the school year. This contributes to the uncertainty urban students face daily and the unpredictability I discussed in previous chapters. Urban school teachers should consider this just part of the landscape.

For example, in the mid-1990s when I taught in an urban high school, I knew of three siblings who lived at separate residences, even though their school records stated they all lived at the same location. One lived with the biological mother, one lived with the grandmother, while the other lived with the grandmother on the child's father's side of family (all three children had different fathers and surnames). And to complicate matters even more, when the biological mother became upset at one or more of her children, or the adult caregivers, she would make the children come back and live with her. The children could go back to their caregivers once the mother calmed down or after reconciliation had been made between the biological mother and whomever she was upset with. So the students were constantly going back and forth, interchanging residences throughout the school year.

ESTABLISH OPEN LINES OF COMMUNICATION

Whether the student lives with a parent, relative, or in some form of foster care, the teacher must work diligently to establish open lines of communication between the classroom and the student's home, wherever that may be. The distance between a student's home life and school life must be reduced. There are no exceptions to this. Students must know, and understand, the connections between home and school and see a working relationship between the parent and teacher. This relationship between parent and teacher will almost always have to be established by the teacher. In order to understand the reasons why teachers must initiate the relationship with parents, you must first look at the types of parents an urban teacher might encounter.

First, there are the highly engaged parents. These parents will be at every school function, meeting, and event the school sponsors. These parents will answer every call from teachers and will take a very active part in their child's educational development. Students with these type of parents will typically have the least amount of behavioral problems. This segment of the parent population will be the minority encountered throughout an urban school teacher's career.

Second, there are the parents who are truly sincere and want to be more involved, but due to circumstances, they are not. This segment of the parent population usually works two or more low-paying jobs (or possibly receives government assistance), may be a single parent (usually a woman), and often has multiple children. These "parents" could also be elderly grandmothers who have taken on the task of raising their grandchildren in order to prevent them from being homeless or having to go to a foster or group home. This segment of the parent population will also be comprised of parents who are dealing with some sort of personal issues that could be overwhelming their lives (i.e., unemployment, spousal abuse, alcohol or drug addiction, juggling school and work, unplanned pregnancy, unexpected deaths in the family, troubles paying bills or buying groceries, or untreated mental or physical illness), therefore putting the school-aged students in a secondary position.

You will find that most of the homes in urban communities are headed by single women with little to no formal education. These parents are aware of the importance of school and want their children to be successful, but they don't perceive themselves as having the time to become actively involved with the school or initiate a relationship with their child's teachers (especially if the child is beyond the elementary grades).

Some may feel intimidated by school officials, or they may feel powerless to some degree. Usually when contacted, they will respond responsibly and will appreciate your attempts to keep them informed. Depending on the school district where you work, this type of parent could be the majority or run a close second to the next parental type.

Lastly, there are the parents and guardians who are neglectful. These are the parents that many teachers loathe. They are neglectful because they do nothing for their children outside of providing food and shelter (and some do not do that adequately). They don't spend time with their children, talk to them, or try to teach them any virtues that will help them in life. These parents can be verbally and physically abusive toward their children. They also model inappropriate behavior and seldom take responsibility for anything that happens. It's always someone else's fault why the child is having issues academically or behaviorally. You will never see this kind of parent at a PTA meeting or parent conference, but chances are, you could see them at a school-sponsored sporting or entertainment event. Parents of this sort almost never have anything good to say about the school or its staff because it's a burden whenever someone from the school contacts them for any reason.

Urban school teachers need to be cautious of this segment of the parent population because they tend to show their disregard for the school in inappropriate ways. They have a tendency to talk loud, use profanity, and can be very disrespectful toward the teacher or any other school employee. This type of parent usually has a lot of personal issues as well (i.e., addiction, unemployment, untreated mental illness, etc.). They make terrible decisions for themselves, and their children usually suffer as a result of their bad decision making.

Students who come from these home situations will typically give teachers the most problems because these are the students who are not used to adhering to any rules or guidelines. These students typically will not have a curfew, will not be required to do homework, and will not accept consequences for their actions. They often suffer verbal or physical abuse from their own parents as well. By the time these children reach the fourth grade, they will have developed a host of socially bad habits and academic deficiencies that are counterproductive to being successful in school (and for society). Unfortunately, urban teachers will experience a great deal of this type of parenting throughout their teaching careers. This type could be the majority or a close second depending on the issues faced by the surrounding community and school district.

In addition to the types of parents an urban teacher may encounter, probably the most profound reason why teachers will have to initiate the relationship with parents is because in urban communities where students live, the adults typically do not trust school officials. The mistrust could have come from the school's history of poor achievement or as a result of the bad experiences the adults had while they were in school themselves. Whatever the case may be, it is because of this mistrust that many parents of urban students stay away from the school, or when they do come, they're combative or in a defensive mode.

Even though there may be a lot of barriers in the way of an urban teacher establishing a relationship with parents, the relationship has to be established nevertheless. Even if the parents are negligent and unwilling, there is somebody out there who cares about the welfare of that student. The classroom teachers have to be persistent and seek that person out. Teachers must hold to the notion that the parent is the first teacher of the child, and both parent and teachers should work cooperatively, and collaboratively, for the benefit of the student.

THE DISCONNECT BETWEEN PARENTS AND TEACHERS

Many urban educators fail miserably in their attempts to make connections with parents because they don't understand that connecting with parents is similar to making connections with students. It involves establishing rapport and relationship building. The process of connecting with parents doesn't happen overnight. Teachers must work systematically in order to establish the relationship and make it work.

Another reason why teachers fail to establish a strong connection with parents of urban students is because they get discouraged easily. When they don't have a working phone number or when they encounter an irate parent over the phone, or in person, they give up. Teachers also have a tendency to give up when they've encountered a parent who, at first glance, seems to be on top of everything, but when it's time for the parent to follow through (i.e., visit the classroom, come to a meeting, volunteer, set routines for the child at home, deliver appropriate consequences to their child, etc.), the parent drops the ball.

Finally, teachers fail to establish contact with parents because of their own negligence. Urban teachers become negligent when they stop including the parent in the child's educational development and stop viewing the parent as an ally. Teachers give up and stop trying when they encounter certain road blocks; but regardless of how nonresponsive parents are, the teacher can't use that as an excuse to leave parents out of the equation. The moment teachers make a conscious decision to stop including parents in the educational development of students, they make a fatal error. Teachers shouldn't let the neglectful actions of a few parents carry over to all parents.

Being an urban school teacher is not an easy task. They have to wear many different hats and are held accountable for student achievement as do teachers who don't have the same student behavioral issues. Urban school teachers can easily find themselves inundated with many task and issues throughout the school day, and some may pop up out of nowhere. Not being prepared will have a teacher constantly reacting to situations.

Unprepared teachers will be reacting to students, parents, administrators, and everyone else in between. In this reactionary state, teachers are allowing the environment to have an impression on them, instead of them making an impression on their environment. In this state, the teacher will be overwhelmed with classroom and school issues, causing the teacher to feel he or she has little time to effectively reach out to parents.

In chapter 2, I discussed the importance of getting to know the students' home environment. The information attained will also help teachers gain an understanding of the adults (parents) in the communities. In many cases when you work in an urban community, you'll be working with the children of the oppressed and downtrodden segment of society. The system has failed them on so many fronts.

They don't have faith in most institutions, especially those they don't completely understand. Many families in these communities suffer from generational poverty and the effects thereof. The greatest problem you will find within the parent population is a feeling of hopelessness. They don't believe they can change things. They don't believe they have a say in issues that affect them and their children.

They don't believe they can make a difference. This is the source of the parents' frustration and anger.

MAKING CONNECTIONS WITH PARENTS

In order to establish a strong relationship with parents of urban students, teachers must act strategically. Their actions must be planned and calculated. Teachers must also be persistent and diligent in trying to make the parent–teacher relationship work. Most students with behavioral issues in school rely on the disconnection between the parents and teachers so they can continue acting in an inappropriate manner. The disconnect prevents them from having any real consequences for their behavior and actions. Some students misbehave in school, go home, and their parent(s) never hears about it because the teacher fails to make any home contact. Some of the students would shape up instantly if their parents, or a concerned adult close to the student, knew what was going on in school on a regular basis.

Before any contact is made to any parent, teachers should ask themselves the following questions:

- What is the best way to communicate with parents?
- What type of information are parents most interested in?
- How often should I attempt to make contact with parents?
- How can the parents and I work together for the benefit of their child?
- What kind of relationship do I want to have with the parents of my students?
- When is it necessary to contact parents about student issues? When is it not?
- In what ways will I attempt to keep parents informed about what's going on in my classroom?

These questions, and those like them, are meant to get urban teachers thinking about parental engagement and serve as the foundation for forming a strategic plan of action. Once you have given the above questions some serious thought, then you will be able to move in the right direction. In order to get the best results from parents, urban teachers must follow the following steps:

- Initiate the contact early and often
- Contact parents when something good happens
- Do not take ownership of things that are beyond your control
- Acknowledge the parents whenever possible.

Not only is initiating parental contact important for urban school teachers, but the frequency of the contact is of equal importance. Teachers should start the contact early in the school year. Before the first day of school, teachers should send a letter to parents introducing themselves and indicating how excited they are to be working with them and their children.

By the end of the first week, another letter should go out. This letter could explain the curriculum, grading, and attendance procedures and how to access class materials and information online and present an overview of classroom and school rules or other information. Make sure that both letters are brief and to the point. It is also a good idea to give the letters a little personalization. Use colored paper or customize your labels. I once knew of a teacher who had her photo printed in the top left-hand corner of the letterhead, so parents would be able to put a face with a name. Customizing the materials you send out to parents will increase the likelihood that the letters will actually be read.

At the end of the second week, leading into the third, teachers should plan to make at least one phone call to the home of every student on their class roster. By this time, the teacher should be a little familiar with the students. Some assignments would have been given, and the teacher would have had a chance to observe students' behaviors and academic skill levels. The main purpose of this call is to merely allow the parent to hear the teacher's voice and to gain some distinction and familiarity.

The teacher should sound friendly, conversational, and enthusiastic. Teachers should never bring up anything negative about the child during this initial phone conversation. The conversation should be light and noncontroversial. The phone call can also be used to clarify items mentioned in the previous letters sent home or to discuss your overall philosophy about education. Before disconnecting the call, teachers should convey the message to parents that they will rely heavily on their assistance to make the educational experience in class a meaningful one for their child.

This approach will initially shock the parent, especially if the child is beyond the elementary school grades, because there are very few urban school teachers they will have encountered that have reached out to them in such a consistent manner. This will serve as the teacher's foundation for building trust and the ground work for establishing rapport. After the teacher has called the parent(s) of every student, the next step would be to select one day in the week that will be designated for contacting parents.

When I was a high school teacher, I called at least five parents every Thursday during my planning period or after school, in addition to the parents of students I contacted regarding behavioral issues. This was a major piece of my classroom management effectiveness. Even if the parent wasn't available, I left a brief message outlining the purpose for my call, and I left information on how to contact me.

When trying to establish rapport with parents, teachers have to become a constant presence, almost like an extension of the family. The increased awareness of the school and the teacher will allow the parent to relax and to drop any defense mechanisms. Many parents become defensive when teachers or school officials call the home. To them, a call home from a school official usually means something is wrong or that the child is in trouble.

Some parents only receive word on how their child is doing after grades come out and the child is failing, or right before the child is about to be suspended from school. This puts the parents in defense mode and makes them more distrustful of the school and its staff. Frequent contact not only keeps parents informed of the student's progress or lack thereof, but it also gives the parents an opportunity to work on trying to resolve the issues with their children.

Leaving the parents out of the loop is definitely a mistake. Teachers should not only call early and often, but they should also contact parents when something good happens. Parents get tired of hearing bad news all the time about their children. Even though the bad news may be totally true, they still may not want to hear it in some cases. Some parents have a hard time acknowledging that their children may have a different personality while away from home. Parents will always have a tendency to only see the goodness in their children.

So during those times when teachers need to call bearing bad news, it is a good practice for teachers to have at least one good thing to say even when the call is for a negative situation. The one positive point can be something the child did in class or something the child did for someone else. It doesn't matter what it is, just as long as it's positive. The positive comment will make the parent more receptive when having to listen to a negative behavioral report. Over time, the parent will see that the teacher is not one sided, and that the teacher is truly trying to work with parents for the student's well-being.

Make sure that when talking to parents you speak clearly and accurately about the situation. Make sure your tone of voice is calm and conversational. Parents should never get the feeling that teachers are talking down to them. Also, make sure you outline to parents what you need from their children in order for them to be successful in the classroom. You will also need to discuss potential consequences the student will face if the behavior doesn't change. This way the parent is fully aware of what's going on and will not be surprised when consequences happen in the future.

AN ALTERNATIVE FORM OF PARENTAL CONTACT

An alternative to making a lot of phone calls is to send positive postcards. As a teacher, I used to send out positive postcards when students did well on a test or did something significant in class. I also used the positive postcards when my schedule didn't allow me to sit down and make calls. I would write a few positive words on the postcard and mail it to the parents. Some parents would call me back immediately after receiving it, while others would not. But the majority of the parents acknowledged they did receive the postcards whenever they actually spoke to me in person. Some parents even shared with me that they saved the postcards and used them as a catalyst for discussing school-related issues with their child.

Another alternative form of parental contact is to make home visits. Some school districts have a visiting teacher on the payroll whose job is to visit the homes of students for various reasons (i.e., truancy, grades, behavior, etc.). If your school district has such a position, make a request for a home visit to be made. If your school district doesn't have such a position, then you should consider making the visit yourself. Doing so will send a strong message to both the parents and the student whom you're visiting that you (the teacher) are passionate about education and that you want the best for the student. I'm not advocating that teachers visit the homes of every student they deliver instruction to each day. The home visit will mostly be reserved for the Extreme Supreme students, as a measure for making connections with them and curbing their behavioral issues.

The home visit may also help you identify concerned individuals in the student's life when the parents are unreachable. Sometimes the teacher's contact (i.e., postcards, phone calls, voice mail messages, letters, etc.) will go unanswered. Sometimes, even a home visit will not put you in direct contact with the biological parents, but there will always be someone (neighbor, relative, or concerned individual) who will divulge information regarding the student or his or her parents.

For example, I once had a student who misbehaved no matter what interventions and strategies I employed. One day the student's behavior in class was so bad that I decided to make a home visit on the same day of his latest incident. The school day ended at 3:15 p.m., and I was knocking on the student's door by 5:00 p.m. No one answered the door, but one of the neighbors heard me knocking and decided to come out of her apartment and address me.

After I explained who I was and my purpose for being there, the neighbor told me that the mother of the student I was looking for was rarely home. She explained that the mother was addicted to crack cocaine and how her four children practically raise themselves. The neighbor knew the student whom I was looking for, and she told me stories of how the student used to look after his younger siblings while his mother was gone, sometimes for days at a time. The neighbor also told me the name and number of the student's aunt who also had an active role in the student's life. The next day, I called the number given to me and was able to speak to the student's aunt. A conference was scheduled with the aunt and the student. As a result of the conference, the student's behavior instantly improved. In fact, the student and I became rather close, and we still keep in contact with each other to this day.

A WORD OF CAUTION

As urban school teachers make frequent contact with parents and start to build rapport and trust, teachers must beware not to try to take ownership of things that are beyond their control. It is possible that as you become more familiar with certain parents, you will start to learn intimate details about their personal lives. In some cases, an initial call home about a student could end up becoming a counseling session for the parent because the parent has used the call as an opportunity to vent his or her personal frustrations.

Some teachers may find it flattering that a parent of one of their students trusts them enough to share such intimate information about themselves. The parent confiding in the teacher is truly a sign that the teacher has gained the parent's trust, which is a good thing, but the teacher must be mindful not to allow the parent to turn it into something more than what's necessary for the child to be successful in school. From the teacher's standpoint, it is wise not to let the parent–teacher relation cross over into a personal friendship. It's a hard enough task trying to care for the students' needs, and teachers do not need to carry the extra burden of caring for the parents in the same manner.

When teachers try to take ownership of things outside their control, they have a tendency to try and fix things for others. You can't become a crutch for parents. When a person gets him- or herself into a mess, that person is usually the one who will have to get him- or herself out of it. I know it will be hard at times because it is easy to become sympathetic to certain issues and have the motivation to offer help, but you must know when to draw the line.

I have heard of numerous cases involving teachers who blurred the lines with parents and it cost the teachers dearly. I can cite examples when teachers lost money that was never repaid to them. There are other instances when teachers have gone above and beyond the call of duty to provide personal assistance and support, only to have the parents turn against them and accuse the teachers of all kinds of things.

But the biggest reason why teachers should not cross the line with parents is due to the emotional investment. The time, energy, sweat, and emotions an urban teacher will invest in the students is enough. They're going to be plenty of proud moments and disappointments associated with the students. Taking on the task of the parents is the quickest way to burn out and exiting the profession prematurely.

Keep the relationship strictly about the students. If you want to help the parents, give them information they can act on, but don't do the work for them. For example, I've informed parents about where to get refurbished computers, vouchers for food and clothes, and where to get free tutoring services, just to name a few. In each case, I merely gave the parents information and let them do the work. This way the parents can continue to take ownership of their own matters.

TRY TO ACKNOWLEDGE PARENTS WHENEVER POSSIBLE

The last point I'd like to make about establishing parental contact is one that is often overlooked by most teachers, doing something special to acknowledge the presence of parents when they show up for a school function. This is overlooked because most educators don't think they should do anything special as an incentive for parents to become involved in their own child's education. This might be true for some parents in more affluent school districts, but when you're talking about urban education, you're dealing with entirely different circumstances. Due to the evasive, transitive, and oftentimes distant nature of parents of urban students, teachers have to be very creative on how they "wheel them in." The upside is that once they get the parents on board, the parents will be the single greatest asset an urban school teacher can have. The following are some positive ways to acknowledge parents:

- Give out parent awards or certificates
- Allow parents to volunteer in the school
- Send thank you letters or postcards
- Applaud parents during assemblies and other meetings
- Allow parents the opportunity to sponsor clubs or events
- Offer incentives for the first fifty parents to show up for a school-sponsored event.

The above list is not an exhaustive one. The main idea behind acknowledging parents is to make them feel good about the school and the role they play in their student's educational development. If parents feel good about the school, they will want to become involved. The greater the presence parents have within the school and classroom, the less likelihood teachers will have behavioral issues from students.

CHAPTER SUMMARY POINTS

- Parents of urban students generally distrust school officials.
- Teachers must work diligently to gain parents' trust and establish rapport.
- Teachers should be the ones to initiate contact with parents.
- Parent contact should be made early and often.
- When calling parents, try to have at least one positive thing to say about the student.
- The types of contact should vary (letters, phone calls, conferences, etc.).
- Don't take ownership of things that are beyond your control.
- Teachers should acknowledge parents when they show up for school functions.

6

CREATING
INTERESTING LESSONS

The final component of successful classroom management skills with little to no behavioral problems is truly the most important one. This aspect of good classroom management practice is the final piece of the puzzle that makes all other efforts outlined in the previous chapters complete. This component calls for all urban school teachers to adequately perform the primary function they are paid to do, and that's to *teach effectively*.

What I'm about to say might offend some educators and may not be the politically correct thing to say, but many urban educators are not adequately teaching urban students or they have a false notion of what real teaching and learning is and what it looks like in action. I've observed over my career in education (both as a teacher and administrator) that the teachers who have the most student behavioral problems, and the worst classroom management skills, are usually the teachers who deliver the poorest quality of instruction.

Their instructional design (lesson planning, instructional delivery, maximization of instructional time, and overall organization) can only be described as being weak and inadequate. The quality of instruction is poor because there is a lack of thought and planning put into lessons. When you add in a lack of knowledge about the students, no established routines, ambiguous rules and consequences (if any at all), and no parental involvement, you get a recipe for disaster. Teachers who fall into this category place an overemphasis on worksheets, lecturing, note taking, watching movies (usually not related to any relevant standard or objective), crossword puzzles, and reading the textbook and answering the end of chapter questions. I'm not saying that teachers should never use any of the above, but the above mentioned items should not be the focal point of a teacher's instructional delivery day after day, month after month, and year after year.

I've also observed many teachers in this category use the "banking model" of education within their classrooms. In the book titled *Pedagogy of the Oppressed*, author Paulo Friere (2000) compared education of the oppressed segment of society to modern-day banking systems. In dealing with banks, the account holder (the one with the money) makes deposits and withdrawals from his or her account. Likewise, in most urban educational systems, the teacher is the account holder with all the knowledge and makes deposits into the students.

In this scenario, there isn't any dialogue, sharing of ideas, meaningful exchanges of information, or transference of knowledge. The banking model of education is outdated and not applicable for today's students. Urban students, like all students, need lessons that will allow them to explore, challenge, and create. They need opportunities to dialogue and to grapple with concepts that will build on prior knowledge and expand their thinking. They need the mental tools to think critically and not be told what is important or what should be regarded as meaningful knowledge.

Good behavior and a good lesson go hand in hand. If the students are engaged in learning, then behavioral problems become a nonissue. Most students in urban classrooms act out merely because they're bored and not appropriately challenged. We live in the most stimulating time in our society. Today's students are not only being entertained by the use of advanced video game technology, multiuse cellular phones, electronic devices, and the Internet, but they are also bombarded with thousands of messages and stimulating images per day via television and radio. Then when they go to school, they encounter a boring teacher who teaches in a boring manner.

For many students, misbehaving in class is merely something to do in order to pass the time. It's unfortunate but in most classes urban students attend, teachers have reduced the lessons to busy work. Busy work is not engaging, challenging, or rigorous. After a short time period, students will put aside the busy work and elect to do something more exciting. What students elect to occupy their time during class usually turns out to be something that will lead to behavioral issues and poor classroom management on behalf of the teacher. This is also the fastest way students lose respect for the teacher.

Remember, in poor neighborhoods, respect and authority is not transferred to a person based on his or her title or credentials. Respect is earned based on a person's actions. Students make judgments about teachers based on the caliber of work teachers place before them. If the work lacks thought, is not appropriately challenging, or does not interest the students, the students will interpret this as a lack of caring on the teacher's behalf. If teachers don't care, then the students will not care either. Once students think teachers don't care about them, then the battle is lost. Students will not show the teachers any respect, behavioral problems will increase, and no meaningful learning will take place. When this happens, the students pay the greatest price.

CREATE ENGAGING LESSONS

Student engagement starts with the teacher's instructional design (Mastropieri and Scruggs, 2000). In order to keep urban students engaged and to maximize instructional time, urban school teachers must master two very important elements of instructional design: creating interesting lessons and having a commanding presence during instructional delivery. These two components will not only increase student achievement and academic performance, but they will also help curtail most behavioral issues.

Creating interesting lessons starts with planning. Lesson planning is arguably the single most important task associated with teaching. There are many different lesson plan templates accepted by various school districts across the country. Some of the best models are constructed as follows:

- Warm-up: This is usually a question or problem used to jump-start the class. It's typically used to get students focused and ready for the day's activities. Warm-ups introduce new materials or reinforce subject matter previously covered. This activity is done during the first ten to fifteen minutes of class.
- Standards: Standards are the state-approved academic content teachers are supposed to teach. It is the content that will be covered in the state-approved test.
- Objectives: These are the goals teachers want students to reach in order to meet the standards. This is what students are expected to learn. Objectives are what students will be able to do after the lesson is over.
- Activities: Classroom activities are the work students will do in order to meet the standards and objectives. These should take the various learning styles of students into account. This includes any materials used, skills students should learn, and exercises to be completed.
- Closure: The culminating activity of any given lesson. Used at the end to emphasis a specific point or to reiterate important points before students exit the classroom. This is completed during the last ten to fifteen minutes of class.

Teachers should take time to structure lessons according to this model or one similar to it. It is also good practice to post the standards and objectives on the board daily and reference them throughout the lesson. Doing so sets clear expectations for what students are expected to do and further entrenches them in the learning process.

One final note about lesson planning: teachers should take into account the various learning styles of students. There are five commonly recognized learning styles that teachers should become familiar with. According to Wentzel (2003), the five most common learning styles are kinesthetic (deals with learning through motion and movement), tactile (deals with learning through touch), social/ interpersonal (involves learning through collaboration and sharing), auditory (involves learning through speaking or debating), and visual (deals with learning through observation).

Teachers who have gained a keen understanding of their students will know the best ways their students learn and will create lessons and instructional activities that match the students' learning styles accordingly and will attack students' deficiencies and improve student achievement. The instructional activities should be varied from day to day or according to the unit or theme being worked on in class. Exposing students to multiple ways to reach the academic goals and objectives will break the monotony and make learning exciting for students.

As mentioned earlier, many urban school teachers make the mistake of oversaturating their lessons with lecturing, note taking, crossword puzzles, and preprinted worksheets. These items should be used as supplemental materials, if at all. Urban school teachers need to structure lessons that allow students to work collaboratively in groups, dialogue with one another, analyze data, fact find, interpret ideas or concepts, use technology, and make presentations.

Many urban school teachers do not have these components as part of their instructional design for two main reason. First, they don't have the confidence to use them. They haven't utilized any of the strategies outlined in this book, so they're not prepared nor are they equipped to deliver high levels of instruction. They don't know any relevant background information on the students, so they are unable to connect with them in a genuine way.

The second reason is associated with fear. They are afraid that something will happen if students start moving around. They are afraid that they will lose control of the class. They are afraid of the potential noise level. They are afraid an administrator will come into the room during the interaction, and the list goes on and on. Urban school teachers need to shed the garment of fear and become more assertive and confident. The strategies outlined in this and previous chapters of this book will help teachers gain the confidence needed to deliver effective lessons to students.

Another element of instructional design that teachers must master is having a commanding presence in class. This means that the teacher is confident, visible, and accessible to students during the lesson. The confidence comes from having a sure understanding of the content and being equipped to handle any behavioral issue that may arise. Most behavioral problems from students can be reduced when teachers are visible and accessible to students.

One of the biggest mistakes a teacher can make is to sit behind a desk or remain at the front of the room next to the door. When this happens, it creates increased opportunities for students to misbehave and go off task. Teachers are unable to monitor students' activities from such positions, which will increase their ineffectiveness. Teachers need to move around the room and circulate among the students. The mere presence of the teacher will curb behavioral problems and allow the teacher to redirect students more quickly.

CHAPTER SUMMARY POINTS

- Teachers shouldn't make worksheets, lecturing, note taking, and crossword puzzles the main part of their instructional design.
- Students need exciting lessons that will allow them to explore, work collaboratively with others, and analyze.
- It is a good practice to post the standards and objectives on the board daily and to reference them throughout the lesson.
- Fear and lack of confidence are the main reasons why some urban teachers teach according to traditional models of instruction.
- Teachers need to have a commanding presence during class.
- Teachers need to circulate around the room during the lesson.

CONCLUSION

This book was written to give teachers a framework for successfully managing their classrooms and for dealing with the most challenging student behaviors. As teachers work with students and attempt to implement the strategies mentioned, I'd like them to keep one thing in mind: students are people too. The statement might seem blatantly obvious, but it's something that urban school teachers must always keep at the forefront of their minds.

I say this because all people—rather young or old—want to be respected, treated fairly, and have a say in the things that matter to them. No one really wants to be told what to do all the time, or made to "follow orders" without being able to express their feelings, concerns, or questions. All teachers, whether they work in an urban school district or not, must realize that effective classroom management is not something that you do to students, but rather something you do with students. Students "experience" classroom management like they do everything else in life.

As human beings, we experience life with every waking moment. Compulsory public education is just one part of a student's many experiences. One of the best ways that teachers are able to enhance the educational experiences within the classroom is by having effective classroom management skills.

Many people believe that effective classroom management is about "keeping students quiet" and "in linc." They believe that unless they control every aspect of the students' movements, they're not doing a good job. The truth is that effective classroom management is not about having the exact answer for every misbehavior students display, administering punishment, striking fear into students, nor is it about having tactics for control.

The best classroom managers understand that interacting, engaging, and understanding students is just as important, if not more important to teaching and learning, than the establishing of routines, rules, and consequences. Teachers who are able to engage students in the experience of learning will be the ones who will have the least amount of student behavioral issues, and the most overall success.

Last, it is a common and well-accepted fact in education that students will misbehave from time to time regardless of how effective the classroom teacher is. It's just a natural part of the educational landscape. Teachers can't control or predict what students will do from day to day, week to week, or year to year; but they can control how they respond to students' misbehaviors. Urban school teachers must be mindful of how they respond to students: their tone of voice, demeanor, gestures, and mannerisms are all important factors. Even if a student is acting belligerent, it doesn't mean that the teacher should meet the student at their level.

Teachers are the paid professionals, so they must act accordingly. Teachers should also reflect on how they handled previous situations involving students' misbehaviors. They should evaluate whether or not they took the right course of action or not. Even if a teacher chose not to respond to a particular misbehavior, they should ask themselves whether or not it was the right thing to do. This would help teachers to become more empathic to students, and more responsive if similar behaviors were to occur in the future.

Being a teacher is not an easy task, especially in this country's current educational climate. I commend all educators who want to devote their careers to helping children learn. To be good at teaching requires a lot of time, energy, patience, understanding, passion, and love. Successfully managing a classroom full of students will not be easy, but it is my sincere hope that this book will serve as a resource used to enhance teachers' knowledge about why students misbehave and to improve their ability to deal with behavioral issues as they occur.

This book will help teachers navigate through the most trying times. Even though some of the strategies mentioned might sound a little unconventional, none of them will fail. All of the strategies are necessary and relevant to the types of students and experiences you'll have as an urban school teacher. This book will not only serve as your guide for better classroom management, but it will also be the foundation for becoming a successful teaching professional as long as you chose to stay in the profession.

BIBLIOGRAPHY

Bianco, A. 2002. *One Minute Discipline: Classroom Management Strategies that Work*. San Francisco: Jossey-Bass.

Blankstein, A., Cole, R., and Houston, R. 2007. *Engaging Every Learner*. Thousand Oaks, CA: Corwin.

Bonnie, D. 2006. *How to Teach Students Who Don't Look Like You*. Thousand Oaks, CA: Corwin.

Brown, D. 2003. Urban Teachers' Use of Culturally Responsive Management Strategies. *Theory Into Practice* 42 (4): 277.

Burden, P. R. 2003. *Classroom Management: Creating a Successful Learning Community*, 2nd ed. New York: Wiley.

Canter, L., and Canter, M. 2001. *Assertive Discipline: Positive Behavior Management for Today's Classroom*, 3rd ed. Los Angeles: Canter.

Corbett, D., Wilson, B., and Williams, B. 2002. *Effort and Excellence in Urban Classrooms: Expecting, and Getting, Success with All Students*. New York: Teachers College Press.

Friere, P. 2000. *Pedagogy of the Oppressed*. New York: Continuum.

Gremler, D., and Gwinner, K. 2008. Rapport-Building Behaviors Used by Retail Employees. *Journal of Retailing* 84 (3): 308–324.

Groves, E. 2009. *The Everything Classroom Management Book*. Avon, MA: Adams Media.

Hess, F. 1999. *Spinning Wheels: The Politics of Urban School Reform*. Washington, DC: Brookings Institution Press.

Hess, F., ed. 2005. *Urban School Reform: Lessons from San Diego*. Cambridge, MA: Harvard Education Press.

Hill, P., and Celio, M. 1998. *Fixing Urban Schools*. Washington, DC: Brookings Institution Press.

Johnson, L., Finn, M., and Lewis, R. 2005. *Urban Education with an Attitude*. New York: State University of New York Press.

Jones, F. 2007. *Tools for Teaching*. Fred H. Jones and Associates.

Jones, V., and Jones, L. 2007. *Comprehensive Classroom Management: Creating Communities of Support and Solving Problems*. Boston: Pearson, Allyn, and Bacon.

Kaiser, B., and Rasminsky, S. 2007. *Challenging Behavior in Young Children*. Boston: Pearson Education.

Kanpol, B. 2002. *Teacher Education and Urban Education*. New York: Hampton Press.

Kraut, H. 2000. *Teaching and the Art of Successful Classroom Management*. Staten Island, NY: AYSA Publishing.

Kunjufu, J. 1986. *Motivating and Preparing Black Youth for Success*. Chicago: African Images.

Kunjufu, J. 2000. *Developing Positive Self-Images and Discipline in Black Children*. Chicago: African Images.

Kunjufu, J. 2002. *Black Students and Middle Class Teachers*. Chicago: African Images.

Lumsden, L. 1998. Teacher morale. ERIC Digest 120. Retrieved from http://eric.uoregon.edu/publications/digests/digest120.html

Macciomei, N., and Ruben, D. 1999. *Behavioral Management in the Public Schools: An Urban Approach*. Westport, CT: Praeger.

Mastropieri, M., and Scruggs, T. 2000. *The Inclusive Classroom: Strategies for Effective Instruction*. Columbus, OH: Merrill.

McAdams, D. 2000. *Fighting to Save Our Urban Schools and Winning*. New York: Teachers College Press.

Mendler, A. 2000. *Motivating Students Who Don't Care: Successful Techniques for Educators*. Bloomington, IN: Solution Tree.

Noguera, P. A. 2003. Schools, prisons, and social implications of punishment: Rethinking disciplinary practices. *Theory Into Practice* 42 (4).

Payne, R. 2005. *A Framework for Understanding Poverty*. Highlands, TX: Aha Process.

Payne, R. 2006a. *Discipline Strategies for the Classroom: Working with Students*. Highlands, TX: Aha Process.

Payne, R. 2006b. *Working with Parents and Building Relationships for Student Success*. Highlands, TX: Aha Process.

Peters, S. 2000. *Inspired to Learn: Why We Must Give Children Hope*. Marietta, GA: Rising Sun Publications.

Quinn, E. 2008. Improve your sport performance with visualization techniques: Guided imagery may improve athletic performance. Retrieved from http://sportsmedicine.about.com/cs/sport_psych/a/aa091700a. htm

Sprick, R. 1985. *Discipline In the Secondary Classroom: A Problem-by-Problem Survival Guide*. West Nyack, NY: Center for Applied Research in Education.

Sprick, R. 2002. *Discipline in the Secondary Classroom*, 2nd ed. San Francisco: Jossey-Bass.

Tickel-Degnen, L., and Rosenthal, R. 1990. The nature of rapport and its nonverbal correlates. *Psychological Inquiry* 1 (4): 285–93.

Tucker, C. 1999. *African American Children: A Self-Empowerment Approach to Modifying Behavior Problems and Preventing Academic Failure*. Boston: Allyn & Bacon.

Weiner, L. 2003. Why is classroom management so vexing to urban teachers? *Theory Into Practice* 42 (4).

Wentzel, K. 2003. Motivating students to behave in socially competent ways. *Theory Into Practice* 42 (4).

Wiles, J., and Bondi, J. 1998. *Curriculum Development: A Guide to Practice*. Upper Saddle River, NJ: Prentice-Hall.

Wood, T., and McCarthy, C. 2002. Understanding and preventing teacher burnout. ERIC Digest. ED477726. Retrieved from http://www.ericdigests.org/2004-1/burnout.htm

Wootan, F., and Mulligan, C. 2009. *Not in My Classroom: A Teacher's Guide To Effective Classroom Management*. Avon, MA: Adams Media.

ABOUT THE AUTHOR

Dr. Sean B. Yisrael began his career in 1998 as a high school social studies teacher. In 2004 he moved into the ranks of school administration, having previously worked in school districts located in Ohio and Washington, D.C. Dr. Yisrael has also worked on the postsecondary level as an adjunct professor at both National College (Ohio) and Trinity University (District of Columbia).

Dr. Yisrael specializes in writing books on teacher and principal effectiveness. Some of his current publications are *The Positive Impact Interdisciplinary Teaming Has On Teacher Morale* (2009); *The 12 Laws of Urban School Leadership* (2012); *and The Hard Truth: Problems, Issues, and People Affecting the Urban School Principalship* (2013). Other soon-to-be-released titles include *The 12 Laws of Effective Teaching; The Warrior Principal; and The Cleopatra Instructor: Effective Teaching Practices from the Ancient Queen of the Nile.*

In 2009, Dr. Yisrael and his wife formed Educational Practitioners for Better Schools (E.P.B.S.), a professional development company designed to provide training and enrichment services to education professionals of all levels. Dr. Yisrael is a highly sought after presenter and has made many speeches and presentations all across the country. He believes that one of the best ways to improve schools is to have well-trained professionals working within them. He has dedicated his life's work to ensure that all students, regardless of their ethnic background or socioeconomic status, receive a quality education in America.

If you would like information about inviting Sean Yisrael to speak to your group, please contact him at www.epbstraining.com or by email at info@epbstraining.com.

CPSIA information can be obtained at www.ICGtesting.com
Printed in the USA
BVOW070646260112

281404BV00002B/3/P

9 781610 487634